Problem-Based Learning in Social Studies
Cues to Culture and Change

Valerie Hastings Moye

SkyLight
Training and Publishing Inc.

Problem-Based Learning in Social Studies: Cues to Culture and Change

Published by SkyLight Training and Publishing Inc.
2626 S. Clearbrook Dr., Arlington Heights, IL 60005
800-348-4474 or 847-290-6600
Fax: 847-290-6609
info@iriskylight. com
http://www.iriskylight.com

Senior Vice President, Product Development: Robin Fogarty
Manager, Product Development: Ela Aktay
Acquisitions Editor: Jean Ward
Project Coordinator: Amy Kinsman
Editor: Dara Lee Howard
Graphic Designer: Heidi Ray
Cover Designer and Illustrator: Dave Stockman
Production Supervisor: Bob Crump
Type Compositor: Donna Ramirez
Proofreader: Jill Oldham
Indexer: Candice Cummins Sunseri

ISBN 1-57517-084-1
LCCCN 98-61159

Item number 1675
07 06 05 04 03 02 01 00 99 98 15 14 13 12 11 10 9 8 7 6 5 4 3 2 1

Contents

Introduction

Section One
Foundation Learning Experiences

Section Two
Culture and Its Components

Section Three
Forces of Change

Section Four
Comparing and Contrasting Cultures

Section Five
Tools of Cultural Study

Section Six
Creating a Museum Display

Acknowledgment

Special thanks are expressed to the Center for Gifted Education at the College of William of Mary in Williamsburg, Virginia. Through the leadership of Dr. Joyce VanTassel-Baska and her staff, problem-based learning has come alive in hundreds of classrooms throughout the United States and other countries. I am grateful that I have been one who has had the opportunity to learn from these curriculum visionaries. The thoughtful modeling and scaffolding provided by Dr. VanTassel-Baska and her staff led to the creation of this unit of study.

Introduction

We are not makers of history. We are made by history.

—Martin Luther King, Jr.

Change and Culture

It is an inescapable truth that students will be the future leaders and problem solvers in a world characterized by diversity, rapid change, and uncertainty. Progression of the democratic society will depend upon how they think and respond to their world. Indeed, an understanding of history and social sciences is important to the development of citizens who will nurture and expand the principles of democracy.

Social studies, or the study of history, geography, civics, and economics, provides a rich story of the events that have shaped lives and the underlying forces that have shaped those events. Throughout this nation's history, great leaders have urged people to learn from the lessons of the past. One of the earliest patriots, Patrick Henry, stressed the importance of studying the past. "I have but one lamp by which my feet are guided, and that is the lamp of experience. I know of no way of judging of the future but by the past." More recently, Martin Luther King, Jr. reiterated Henry's sage advice when he pointed out that people are what history has made them to be.

Often, however, students bog down in the details of history and do not see its thrust and direction—the big picture of how or why the story unfolded. Thus, social studies has little significance to students who are expected to master details rather than concepts. Without a context in which to acquire an understanding of why it is important to learn about the past, students disengage from learning that could be most meaningful—an understanding of how humans continue to survive through prosperity and adversity.

This book presents a social studies unit designed to actively engage elementary students in learning many of the facts, skills, and concepts that serve as a foundation for understanding culture and the influence of change. To prepare students to respond to a world characterized by diversity and transformation, the unit examines the concepts of culture and change, using ancient Egypt as an example. Students learn essential skills of problem solving, develop an understanding of the forces that define and shape all cultures, and form a conceptual foundation for the extended study of other ancient or modern cultures. The unit is the first step in a continuous study that could extend through the social studies curriculum for K–12 learners.

Although the unit addresses ancient Egypt and the modern U.S. classroom as its counterpoint, the mode of study is infinitely adaptable to other social studies units. Teachers are encouraged to adapt both curricular models and implementation activities to a variety of topics, thus enriching students' grasp of the major concepts and skills.

How This Book Is Organized

The remainder of this introduction includes background information for implementing this unit. Two critical teaching models that provide the structure of the unit are discussed and are used to introduce the targeted content. The curricular model discussion is followed by an examination of unit implementation concerns, ranging from prerequisites to assessments. An overview of the format of the learning experiences is provided.

The next section sets the foundation for the unit with four learning experiences that establish key basic knowledge for the unit. Foundation experiences are followed by sections 3 to 7, which present learning experiences for each of five learning objectives, including summative as well as informal assessment rubrics. There are two appendices, one for resources and one for notes about ancient Egypt.

Curricular Models

This unit incorporates *concept-based teaching* and *problem-based learning* to actively engage students in examining the underlying forces that shape cultures and the historical events such cultures ultimately produce. Successful implementation of the unit depends upon the successful use of these interactive learning experiences. A brief review of the basic characteristics of these two curricular models serves as a foundation for understanding how to implement this unit.

SkyLight Training and Publishing Inc.

Concept Teaching: Linking Facts to Structures and Big Ideas

Two powerful concepts, culture and change, target ten broad ideas and provide a basis for five unit objectives.

Two Concepts

What, exactly, is a concept? In the simplest of terms, a concept is an eternal truth, issue, or controversy. In a lecture during the Curriculum for the Gifted course at the College of William and Mary, Williamsburg, Virginia, in the spring of 1996, VanTassel-Baska said, "concepts focus on the ideas that have guided the development of civilization as we know it." Concepts are broadly based, overarching, and allow for valid connections within a subject (Center for Gifted Education 1994). Concepts reveal fundamental patterns, similarities, and differences, encourage a deeper examination of subject matter, and stimulate learners' curiosity.

Culture and change are concepts—they reflect these criteria. They also provide an opportunity to span a common theme in the kindergarten through grade 12 social studies curriculum.

Culture

Goodenough (1963) described culture as a mental construct that provides individuals in society with a cognitive map of appropriate rules for behavior in various situations. The study of culture allows students to examine important issues and to relate specific facts to those issues to increase meaning. Spindler (1977) further defined culture as a "sifter of ideas" (5) that are patterned in certain ways to reflect basic assumptions about how the world works. These ideas distinguish one culture from another in terms of their beliefs and their responses to events. In this context, students seek patterns that define similarities among and differences between cultures.

Change

Change also provides a meaningful context in which students can view events documented historically. Smith broadly defined change as "a succession of events which produce over time a modification or replacement of particular patterns or units by other novel ones" (1976, 13). Smith delineated the following qualities of change that are fundamental to the big ideas of culture and change:

1. Change always involves an alteration of some pattern or thing.

2. Change is always temporal as well as spatial.

3. Change is infeasible without movement.

4. Change always involves some reference to events which mark a transition.

5. Change is always change of patterns and units in a particular space and time.

Spindler and Spindler (1959) linked the concepts of culture and change to increase understanding of how these two powerful concepts can be used to organize social studies curriculum and instruction. These authors specifically defined cultural change as ". . . any modification in the way of life of a people, whether consequent to internal developments or to contact between two peoples with unlike ways of life" (37).

These two concepts provide a powerful framework on which to build a social studies curriculum for learners of all ages. One purpose of this book is to outline an initial example of such a curriculum for elementary students.

Ten Big Ideas

The ten big ideas link discrete facts and skills to be learned and are derived from the concepts of culture and change. In essence, the ten ideas are the substance of knowledge that the students acquire through this unit. Posting the big ideas in the classroom and pointing out their relationship to each of the proposed activities is one way to emphasize their importance to students, who could be asked to articulate the relationship of the targeted big ideas to what they are learning.

Five Unit Objectives

Finally, five objectives are identified (see page 6) and linked to the ten big ideas of culture and change. The five objectives used in the unit are appropriate for elementary students and are specifically targeted for high-ability third graders; although, the unit could be adapted for older elementary students. The relationship between the two concepts, the ten big ideas, and these five unit objectives is the crux of the unit and serves to weld the activities into a useful whole.

Beyond the Unit
Culture and change are two overarching concepts that could bridge the social studies curriculum for elementary, middle, and high school students. This could be accomplished through the delineation of objectives that link to the ten big ideas. For example, one overall goal of the social studies curriculum might be

Ten Big Ideas of Culture and Change

 The formation of culture depends on humans' ability to symbolize.

 Every cultural trait has form, meaning, and function.

 Cultures are formed by their members to support survival and to increase quality of life.

 Culture affects the behavior of its members, and its members influence it.

 Culture helps us to describe, explain, and predict behavior for individuals and groups.

 Members of cultures share basic needs: food and shelter to survive and hope and meaning in their lives. All aspects of a culture relate to these needs.

 A culture is made up of many ways of acting and thinking. Some of these ways are changing; some are remaining the same.

 All cultures change, and many factors contribute to change.

 Cultural changes are introduced through both inside and outside sources (i.e., environment, conflict, acculturation, diffusionism, or innovation).

 Cultural changes can be observed and recorded.

Five Unit Objectives

OBJECTIVE 1

Demonstrate an understanding of the concept *culture* and the following related components of cultural study: technology, ideology, sociology, and attitude.

OBJECTIVE 2

Identify evidence of cultural change and causes for change in ancient Egypt as well as in the students' classroom and school.

OBJECTIVE 3

Apply cultural understanding to compare and contrast characteristics of the ancient Egyptian with the students' classroom and school cultures.

OBJECTIVE 4

Describe and apply simple procedures (observations, interviews, and archaeological digs) used by archaeologists, sociologists, and anthropologists to study cultures.

OBJECTIVE 5

Demonstrate an understanding of the occupations, practices, and routines associated with museums as preparation for a comparative display on culture and change in ancient Egypt and in the students' classroom.

SkyLight Training and Publishing Inc.

that students will be able to apply the concept of culture to varied past and present cultural constructs and will be able to identify and analyze possible forces involved in cultural change. Then, specific supporting objectives that link the ten big ideas about the two concepts of culture and change could be identified for elementary, middle, and high school students.

By the completion of grade 5, students should be able to meet these objectives:

- Apply the concept of culture and White's (1959) components of cultural study to analyze new cultures encountered through study

- Interpret the concept of culture as applied to the early colonists in the United States by using cultural components to describe them

- Analyze changes within specific identified cultures

- Analyze those components of early U.S. culture that were borrowed and those that were the result of innovation

- Develop a profile of an innovator

- Analyze the characteristics of U.S. innovators and how they shaped early U.S. culture

- Describe and continue to apply procedures involved in cultural study, such as archaeological excavation, piecing of artifacts, interviewing, and observation

By grade 8, students should be able to achieve these objectives:

- Compare two systems for analyzing cultural components

- Interpret the various schools of cultural change (i.e., evolutionism, diffusionism, acculturation, and neoevolutionism)

- Apply the schools of cultural change to the explanation of changes within specific identified cultures, past and present

- Interpret the concept of culture to explain Hitler's Third Reich and other occurrences that led to World War II

- Interpret the concept of culture as it applies to the economic, social, and political transformation of the United States since World War II, with particular emphasis on the civil rights movement and the changing role of women

- Analyze the impact that early federal policy had on Native American culture and relate to change forces that have influenced cultures previously studied

- Define the characteristics of ethnographies by reading, analyzing, and comparing at least five ethnographies related to the United States and other cultures

- Practice naturalistic observations, interviews, note taking, and data interpretation procedures used in qualitative research

By the completion of grade 12, objectives for students include the following:

- Distinguish past and present sociologists, anthropologists, and archaeologists who have made outstanding contributions to understanding various cultures and change

- Conduct qualitative research on some aspect of school or community life and relate the research to the concept of culture

- Write an ethnography on some aspect of modern culture in the United States

- Discern laws that have influenced cultural change in the United States

- Interpret the United States Constitution's impact on cultural change in the United States

- Predict potential cultural change forces that could affect the United States on the home front and in foreign policy

- Differentiate between artifact dating procedures and continue to apply excavation, observation, interview, and other data interpretation techniques used by sociologists, anthropologists, and archaeologists to study cultures

As can be seen, the initial objectives may be expanded for successively higher grade levels and can be built on continually, providing continuity and meaning to the social studies curriculum.

Problem-Based Learning: Creating Authenticity

The second curricular model incorporates problem-based learning into the unit. This active and integrative curriculum and instruction model is designed "around real-life problems that are ill-structured, open-ended, or ambiguous" (Fogarty 1997, 2). Ill-structured problems are dynamic, offer controversy, resist simple solutions, and require reflection. Such problems engage the students in authentic learning situations that allow for intellectual inquiry and require the use of skills and habits of mind necessary to be successful in the world (Barell 1995). Indeed, "another important overarching feature of PBL is the development, practice, and support of metacognition" (Boyce et al. 1997, 369). As maintained by the Center for Gifted Education at the College of William and Mary, problem-based learning supports "the integration of content, process, and concept learning" through the engagement of students in "realistic problems" (Boyce et al. 1996, 374).

Teacher's Role

Because problem-based learning centers around an ambiguous problem that evolves as students gain insight into what they already know and what they need to know in order to solve the problem, the roles that teachers and students assume often change. Teachers are no longer the "sage on the stage"; instead, they are guides whose primary role is to ask questions that lead students to consider various nuances suggested by the problem. In this role, teachers may develop touchstone teaching and learning events that spur students toward information that may help them solve their problem. Teachers provide minilectures or learning experiences only when students indicate a need to know additional information. However, more often than not, the teacher's role is played through more indirect ways, such as the following:

1. Ask students to clarify their actions or thoughts.

2. Lead students to find information for themselves.

3. Refocus students' pursuits.

4. Evaluate the products and processes of problem solving.

Students' Role

Accordingly, students assume a role as stakeholders of the problem. As stakeholders, they do the following:

1. Define the problem.

2. Gather, share, and create knowledge.

3. Resolve the problem.

4. Evaluate the reasoning, strategies, and solutions that are used to solve the problem.

Problem Statement

Problem-based learning usually is introduced through the use of a problem statement prepared by the teacher (see blacklines for The Problem Statement). Students get their first glimpse of their stakeholder role for the problem from the problem statement. The stakeholder position offers a point of view that is reflected in the problem solution.

Immediately after reading the problem, teacher and students construct a Knowledge Status Chart (see blacklines) by brainstorming three questions: (1) what do students already know about the problem that may help in its solution, (2) what do they need to know to develop a solution to the problem, and (3) how might they obtain the information they need to solve the problem. Students continually revisit this chart and update each section with current status and information.

In this book, the students assume the stakeholder role of a director of a museum. As director, they have the responsibility of preparing and exhibiting a display that celebrates the city's 200th anniversary. The director has been asked to compare the culture of a modern day Memphis school to that of its ancient predecessor. Moreover, the students learn that a great deal is at stake, for there are threats to reduce the funding of the museum to the point that it may be closed.

Unit Implementation

Prerequisites

Students need several prerequisites to engage successfully in this unit.

1. Students need some knowledge of a culture, perhaps one that they have recently studied or about which they have some recent knowledge or experience. In this unit, Native American culture is used as the introductory culture.

2. They also need to be able to read and write with a fair degree of proficiency.

3. Students must be able to work independently as well as in cooperative groups.

4. Finally, students must know how to use various graphic organizers, such as mind maps, Venn diagrams, and classification charts, as well as how to make critical observations.

If students do not possess these skills, then additional scaffolding and guidance from the teacher might be required to adapt the lessons and assist the students.

Section and Learning Experience Formats

Each section is arranged in the same way. It begins with the objective and is followed by relevant learning experiences, which are presented in the same format. As mentioned earlier, the foundation experiences and each objective are presented in individual sections. For each learning experience, the big ideas related to that learning experience are listed, followed by the steps necessary for the learning experience. To quickly find the primary activity or activities for the experience, look for the heart icon next to a step. Finally, the learning experience concludes with a reflection activity that encourages metacognitive processing about some element of the experience.

Scope of Learning Experiences

The very nature of problem-based learning resists the delineation of a specific scope and sequence for the implementation of learning experiences. The learning experiences included here provide students with opportunities to explore the big ideas pertaining to the concepts of culture and change and have been designed to assist students in achieving the objectives; however, many other learning experiences also may be needed. The classroom teacher is in the best position to determine the nature of these learning experiences. Thus, the learning experiences included in this unit serve only as examples of touchstone teaching and learning opportunities that might be implemented. Although the unit predicts certain things that the students will need to know and suggests learning experiences for helping them to obtain that knowledge, do not assume that all learning experiences have been predetermined. Rather, these are suggestions of the kinds of learning experiences that might be provided through an evolving unit that reflects students' knowledge and interests. What students know, need to know, and how they will obtain that knowledge strongly influences a teacher's plan for additional touchstone lessons and methods of finding information.

Sequence of Learning Experiences

Except for completing the foundation experiences in section 2 first, no particular sequence for implementing the remaining learning experiences is required.

That is, presentation of learning experiences need not be restricted to the order used in the book. Teachers need to offer experiences as they are required to accommodate the class' need for knowledge. Let the students' need to know about something guide choices not only within an objective but also between objectives.

Instructional Strategies

Various instructional strategies are used throughout this unit. As indicated earlier, the entire unit embodies problem-based learning. Additionally, students are asked to construct their own knowledge and to think about their own thinking as they engage in the learning activities. To this end, each activity presents an opportunity for student reflection.

Cooperative learning is balanced with individual work. The cooperative learning activities are designed in such a way that students are not used as tutors for one another but are encouraged to engage in reflective dialog through small group pursuits. Accompanying resource activity sheets serve as guides for the cooperative learning groups. Cooperative group work is balanced with individual research and reflection.

The unit has a strong experiential basis as students apply what they learn in contexts that can be assimilated easily. Thus, students engage in researching, observing, recording, and interpreting endeavors that are similar to those accomplished by historians, archaeologists, and anthropologists. Such activities enable the students to bridge their own classroom culture to that of the ancient Egyptians.

Time Frame

Most of the learning experiences take approximately one hour; however, some may take as long as one and a half hours. At least nine weeks are needed to complete the entire unit, and teachers may extend the time to cover a semester if desired. Completion time really depends on how involved the students are in the unit, how the problem-solving strategies evolve, what depth of knowledge teacher and students wish to pursue, and finally, how many additional learning experiences are needed so that students achieve the unit objectives and understand the big ideas of culture and change.

Culminating Learning Experience

The culminating learning experience is the preparation and display of an exhibit that compares ancient Egypt and the students' school culture. It is suggested that this exhibit be placed in the school lobby, an actual museum, or some other public building. It also is recommended that a museum director actually evaluate the final exhibit using the rubric included in the blacklines section.

Assessment Procedures

Summative Assessment

Varied assessments are used to determine whether students have achieved the instructional objectives. Because a seamless connection between curriculum and assessment is desired, the assessment activities are included in each section with the activities for a given objective. In some instances, reflection for a particular activity contains a formalized assessment.

Informal Assessment

Also, more informal assessments are implied for the unit. In particular, students are asked to maintain journals with many guided reflective activities. Responding to such activities provides students an opportunity to assess and evaluate information presented to them. Also, journals give teachers the chance to witness and respond to their students' ideas about presented concepts. As the teacher reads what the students have written and responds in a meaningful way, the students' journals become a useful communication tool.

It is recommended, at the completion of the unit, that the teacher evaluate the students' journals for these characteristics:

1. Completion of reflective activities.

2. Mastery of concepts and ideas presented in lessons.

3. Quality of presentation.

4. Overall quality of reflections.

As with all assessments, the students should be informed in advance that their journals will be assessed and how they will be assessed. This communicates to the students that their journal work is important. A suggested scoring rubric for the students' journals is included in the blacklines section.

SECTION ONE

Foundation Learning Experiences

What Is the Problem?

Related Big Ideas

This learning experience introduces the topic and initiates thinking about the problem. As such, it is indirectly related to all the big ideas but does not directly focus on any particular ones.

What To Do

1. Give students a copy of The Problem Statement (see blacklines).

2. Explain this is a problem they are to solve as a class. They each play the role of a director of a museum and try to solve a problem the director faces.

3. Read the problem statement to the students as they follow along.

4. Display a large piece of chart paper or bulletin board paper with The Knowledge Status Chart (see blacklines) graphic organizer.

 5. Ask the students what they know after reading The Problem Statement (see blacklines). In the column marked Know? write down their comments.

 6. Ask the students what they think they need to know to solve the problem. In the column marked Need-to-Know? write down their comments.

 7. Ask the students how they think they can find information about what they need to know. In the column marked Find Out? write down their comments.

8. Post this chart in the room during the time they are solving the problem. Ask students to update information on the chart as they know more, as they need to know more, and as they find new ways to discover information they need to solve the problem.

9. Both teacher and students refer to the chart as the students solve the problem.

10. Introduce the students to the journal requirement for the project. Share the suggested Journal Scoring Rubric (see blacklines) with students.

Reflection

While completing the chart and throughout problem solving, challenge students to tell specifically how they came up with an idea. For example, in completing the Know? column, if students say "We know the museum might close," ask for the source of that knowledge. How do they know that fact?

What Is Change?*

Related Big Ideas

 A culture is made up of many ways of acting and thinking. Some of these ways are changing; some are remaining the same.

 All cultures change, and many factors contribute to change.

 Cultural changes are introduced through both inside and outside sources (i.e., environment, conflict, acculturation, diffusionism, or innovation).

 Cultural changes can be observed and recorded.

What To Do

1. Explain that students are to think about the concept *change*. It is an important concept needed to develop their museum display.

2. Divide students into cooperative groups of four. Review responsibilities and assign one student to each of these tasks: materials manager, timekeeper and encourager, recorder, and reporter.

3. Ask the materials manager to get a large sheet of chart paper, fold it into fourths, and label it as shown under Change Concept.

* *This learning experience is adapted with permission from Center for Gifted Education, College of William and Mary (1998)* Language Arts Units for High Ability Learners K–8, *Dubuque, IA: Kendall Hunt.*

Change Concept

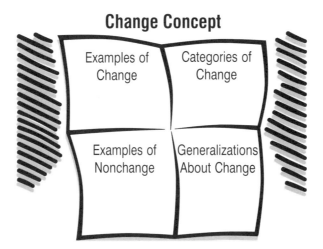

Examples of Change

Categories of Change

Examples of Nonchange

Generalizations About Change

4. Discuss the concept of *change* with the class, noting there are always examples of change in the world. Ask one or two students to give an example of change. Then ask the students, working in their cooperative groups, to brainstorm examples of change and have the recorder write their answers in the Examples of Change block of the chart. Allow five minutes for this task.

5. Ask the reporter with the longest list of examples to share them with the class. Ask recorders in the other groups to check off the same or similar ideas on their lists. Then, ask for examples of change that have not been given. Finally, ask students to examine the examples of change and to provide what they think are some of the characteristics of change.

6. Refer to a few student examples of change that are somewhat similar. Ask the students to suggest a name for a category in which they might place these examples of change. For example, change in hair, change in weight, and change in height could be placed in a category called Physical Change in People. Ask the students to list three to five categories in which they might sort their examples of change. Ask recorders to write the categories in the block marked Categories of Change. Give the students ten minutes to complete this task.

7. After the time is up, ask reporters to tell how their group came up with their categories and tell what the categories are.

8. Next, ask one or two students in the class to tell about something they think does not change. Then, ask students, again working in their cooperative groups, to brainstorm examples of nonchange and have recorders write their ideas in the block designated Examples of Nonchange. Allow five minutes for this task.

9. Ask the reporter with the longest list of examples of nonchange to share them with the class, and have recorders in the other groups check off similar ideas on their lists. Then ask for examples of nonchange that have not been listed.

10. Ask the students which was harder—finding examples of change or nonchange. Also, ask them what, if any, is the difference between the two sets of examples.

11. Ask the class to give a generalization or statement about change that is true and applies to all the examples of change. For example, one generalization might be that change can be good or bad.

12. Ask the cooperative groups to think of other generalizations about change and write down three or four in the block Generalizations About Change. Give the students about ten minutes to do this.

13. Have reporters share their groups' generalizations with the class.

14. Explain there are several generalizations about change and culture that are important to consider as students solve the museum problem, but before examining those generalizations, they must also examine the concept of culture.

Reflection

This entire learning experience calls for reflection and analysis. The graphic organizer documents the cooperative groups' reflections. Ask students to personally reflect on one group discussion item about which they at first disagreed but finally agreed with. What was the key that unlocked their mind to the new idea? Would this key work on persuading someone else to change their mind?

Culture and Its Components

Related Big Ideas

 Every cultural trait has form, meaning, and function.

 Cultures are formed by their members to support survival and to increase quality of life.

 Culture affects the behavior of its members, and its members influence it.

 Members of cultures share basic needs: food and shelter to survive and hope and meaning in their lives. All aspects of a culture relate to these needs.

What To Do

1. Ask students if they have studied Native Americans in school.

2. Brainstorm what they learned when they studied Native Americans and write down their responses on a large piece of paper.

3. Explain what they have just brainstormed is a description of culture.

 4. Ask the students to work in groups of two to three members and write on a large piece of paper what they think the word *culture* means. After about fifteen minutes, bring the groups back together and have them share their definitions.

5. Share the Definition of Culture with the class. Ask the students to tell what their definitions have in common with and how they differ from the shared definition. Have students use the Chart for Comparing Definitions to record their responses (see blacklines).

Definition of Culture

Culture provides a group of people with a map of appropriate rules for behavior in various situations. It includes thought, speech, action, and artifacts and depends on the ability of humans to learn and to pass knowledge to others, especially to succeeding generations.

---

6. Explain if students look at the list of things they have studied about Native Americans, each aspect can be classified in one of four categories: technology, ideas, relationship to one another, and attitudes about the world.

7. Provide a detailed description of these four aspects of cultural study, along with Native American examples.

8. Ask students to play a game using slips of paper on which different aspects of Native American life are written.

   a. For each group, prepare small (2" x 1") strips of paper to use with large poster board divided into four classification areas (see Classification Activity): technology, ideology, sociology, and attitude.

   b. On each strip of paper, students write one word or phrase or sketch a figure that describes Native American life (examples: teepee, arrows, Indian chief, warriors, worshipped nature, etc.).

   c. Students classify the various aspects (the paper strips) according to the four cultural components (the categories on the poster-board chart). The teacher will want to rotate among the groups as the students play the game.

Classification Activity

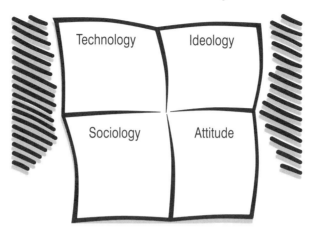

Technology | Ideology

Sociology | Attitude

9. Have a traveler from each group check with other groups on how they are classifying the various aspects of Native American life.

10. Bring the entire class together and ask the various groups to describe their classifications and to explain why they classified as they did.

Reflection

The game gives students an opportunity to reflect on the four components of cultural study. Ask students to imagine they are to explain their classroom culture to a Native American using the same categories. Which category would they consider most important to start with and why?

What Is Culture?

Related Big Ideas

 The formation of culture depends on humans' ability to symbolize.

 Every cultural trait has form, meaning, and function.

 Cultures are formed by their members to support survival and to increase quality of life.

 Culture affects the behavior of its members, and its members influence it.

 Culture helps people describe, explain, and predict behavior for individuals and groups.

 Members of cultures share basic needs: food and shelter to survive and hope and meaning in their lives. All aspects of a culture relate to these needs.

What To Do

1. Ask students to think about the concept of *culture* because it is important for developing their museum display.

2. Divide the students into cooperative groups of four. Assign one student to be the materials manager, one to be the timekeeper and

encourager, one to be the recorder, and one to be the reporter. Review the responsibilities for these tasks.

3. Have the materials manager get a large sheet of chart paper, fold it into fourths, and label as shown in the Culture Chart.

Culture Chart

Signs of Culture	Categories of Signs of Culture
Things That Are Not Part of Culture	Generalizations About Culture

4. Refer to the Definition of Culture used in Culture and Its Components (see also the Chart for Comparing Definitions in the blacklines section.) Ask one or two students to give an example of an aspect of culture. Then ask the students working in their cooperative groups to brainstorm signs of culture and have the recorder write their ideas in the Signs of Culture block. Allow five minutes to complete this task.

5. Ask the reporter with the longest list of examples to share them with the class, and have the recorders in the other groups check off those on their lists that are similar. Then, ask for examples of signs of culture that have not been reported. Finally, ask students to examine the examples of aspects of culture and to provide what they think are some of the characteristics of culture.

6. Refer to two to four examples from the students' signs of culture that are somewhat similar. Ask students for a name of a category in which to place these aspects. For example, in considering the culture of the

United States, the cultural aspects of a birthday party, the Fourth of July, and Thanksgiving Day might be placed in the category "Celebration." Ask students to find two to three categories for all their examples of culture and have the recorder write the categories in the block marked Categories of Signs of Culture. Give the students ten minutes to complete the task.

7. Next, ask reporters to tell how their group came up with their categories and tell what the categories are.

8. Ask one or two students in the class to tell about something they think does not have to do with culture. Then, ask students in their groups to brainstorm examples that are not culture and have the recorder write their ideas in the block designated Things That Are Not Part of Culture. Allow about five minutes to complete the task.

9. The students should have a hard time coming up with examples that are not part of culture. Have the reporter with the longest list of these examples share them with the class as recorders in the other groups check off similar items on their lists. Then, ask for examples that have not been listed.

10. Ask the students why they think it was so hard to find examples that are not part of culture.

11. As a class, ask the students to make a generalization or statement about culture that is true and applies to all the examples of culture. For example, one generalization might be that many things might cause a culture to change.

12. Ask the cooperative groups to think of other generalizations about culture and write down three or four in the block labeled Generalizations About Culture. Give the students ten minutes to come up with these generalizations.

13. Have the reporters share their groups' generalizations with the class.

14. Explain there are several generalizations about change and culture they will consider as they solve the museum problem. Review the Ten Big Ideas of Culture and Change (see introduction). Post the ten big ideas in the classroom as an easy reminder of these generalizations.

Reflection

Backtracking for a moment, ask students to think about what cultural aspects from this learning experience were similar to examples from Culture and Its Components. Which were different? Could aspects from different cultures fit in a category together? Why or why not?

SECTION TWO

Culture and Its Components

OBJECTIVE 1

Demonstrate an understanding of the concept *culture* and the following related components of cultural study: technology, ideology, sociology, and attitude.

Classroom Cultural Components

Related Big Ideas

 Every cultural trait has form, meaning, and function.

 Cultures are formed by their members to support survival and to increase quality of life.

 Culture affects the behavior of its members, and its members influence it.

 Members of cultures share basic needs: food and shelter to survive and hope and meaning in their lives. All aspects of a culture relate to these needs.

What To Do

1. Dress up as an anthropologist. For example, wear a safari hat and a field jacket or shirt.

2. Explain the role of an anthropologist.

3. Review what was learned about culture and the four components of culture. Ask students to relate examples of different aspects of culture in Native American life.

4. Students discuss the following questions:

   a. Are all people part of a culture?

b. Why do you think there is such a thing as culture?

5. Ask students to think about how tools, ideas, roles, and attitudes are related to their questions.

6. Explain classrooms have culture, and ask students to explain how they know their classroom has a culture.

7. Tell the students, as amateur anthropologists, they will look for evidence of the four cultural components in their own classroom.

8. Divide the students into teams to gather evidence of the four cultural components in their classroom. Have students record their findings (see Team Findings in the blackline section). Bring teams together to share their findings.

Reflection

The Team Findings Sheet provides an opportunity for the students to reflect. Using their findings, ask students to draw a diagram of the cultural aspects of their classroom. Which aspects were easy to portray? Which were difficult? Why?

Culture and Symbols in the Classroom

Related Big Ideas

 The formation of culture depends on humans' ability to symbolize.

 Every cultural trait has form, meaning, and function.

 Cultures are formed by their members to support survival and to increase quality of life.

 Culture affects the behavior of its members, and its members influence it.

 Members of cultures share basic needs: food and shelter to survive and hope and meaning in their lives. All aspects of a culture relate to these needs.

What To Do

1. Review previous work about the components of a culture.

2. Ask the students if they think animals have a culture. After some discussion, explain only humans are considered to have a culture because only humans have the ability to symbolize.

3. Ask students what they think a symbol is.

 4. Ask students to give a few examples of symbols from their classroom. Remind students their own classroom can be viewed as a culture.

Brainstorm the various aspects of classroom life. Have the students create symbols for their classroom, representing various aspects of classroom life. Use different materials such as clay, material, paint, buttons, and so forth to produce the symbols.

5. Ask students to write an essay explaining their symbols. Introduce the Scoring Rubric for Cultural Symbols Essay (see blacklines).

Reflection

The essay provides one opportunity for the students to reflect. Use the Scoring Rubric for Cultural Symbols Essay for evaluation. Another question might be to ask students to think about big idea number 4 (Culture affects the behavior of its members and its members influence it) and if they think that they affect their classroom culture. Instruct students to pair up and share thoughts.

Egyptian Cultural Components

Related Big Ideas

 Every cultural trait has form, meaning, and function.

 Cultures are formed by their members to support survival and to increase quality of life.

 Culture affects the behavior of its members, and its members influence it.

 Members of cultures share basic needs: food and shelter to survive and hope and meaning in their lives. All aspects of a culture relate to these needs.

What To Do

1. Dress up as an ancient Egyptian.

2. Review previous work about the components of a culture. Remind students each of the components has many aspects of life related to it.

3. Explain that the class is to study the ancient Egyptian culture, which existed over 5,000 years ago.

4. View a film (*Ancient Lives: Village of the Craftsmen*) that describes that culture. Divide the class into groups and ask each group to take notes on different aspects of the culture using the four components of cultural study.

 5. Divide students into groups and have each group prepare a mind map to share with the class during discussion.

6. Have groups share their mind maps with the class and tell what they learned during the film.

Reflection

The mind maps provide opportunities for reflection as the students apply the classification to examine aspects of cultural study. Ask each student to complete the sentence, "The most interesting thing we learned about the ancient Egyptians was . . . ." Have students share their choices with their groups.

Introduction of Research Project

Related Big Ideas

 The formation of culture depends on humans' ability to symbolize.

 Every cultural trait has form, meaning, and function.

 Cultures are formed by their members to support survival and to increase quality of life.

 Culture affects the behavior of its members, and its members influence it.

 Culture helps people describe, explain, and predict behavior for individuals and groups.

 Members of cultures share basic needs: food and shelter to survive and hope and meaning in their lives. All aspects of a culture relate to these needs.

What To Do

1. Introduce this learning experience by acting as the director of the Children's Museum. You have just been informed that due to a cut in funding, all the Egyptologists needed by the museum cannot be hired. Yet, you must prepare the display. (Note: An alternative might be to

have someone else arrive as the director. This could be a parent, another staff member, etc.)

2. Explain what an Egyptologist is and ask the students to take on the role of Egyptologists.

 3. Announce the research project.

    a. Each student needs to select and research one aspect of Egyptian life to share with the class. Ask students to brainstorm aspects of Egyptian life to research. Ask them to compare their lists to the one under Ancient Egypt Research Topics.

Ancient Egypt Research Topics*

- Agriculture
- Cities, Towns & Villages
- Clothing
- Conflicts
- Economics
- Education

- Food
- Geography
- Houses
- Laws and Legal System
- Leisure
- Medicine

- Mummification/ Burials
- Pharaohs
- Religion
- Resources & Trade
- Roles of Men, Women & Children

*Note: An additional list could be generated around issues and questions.

---

    b. Students use the Guidelines for Research Projects (see blacklines) to collect and report information to the class. Students act as resident experts on their aspects of Egyptian life throughout the project.

    c. Introduce the Research Project Scoring Rubric (see blacklines).

 4. Have the class brainstorm possible resources for their research. Write the resources on a large piece of paper and have students maintain an ongoing list in their journals. This journal activity continues throughout the unit with various reporting due dates assigned.

Reflection

Use the Research Project Scoring Rubric (see blacklines) to assess students'
reports. Ask them to look at the rubric and think about which criteria are
easiest for them to meet and which are the hardest. What can they do to make
the hard ones easier? Ask them to jot a few notes about this in their journals.

SkyLight Training and Publishing Inc.

Symbols and Hieroglyphics

Related Big Ideas

 The formation of culture depends on humans' ability to symbolize.

 Every cultural trait has form, meaning, and function.

What To Do

1. Dress as a scribe.

2. Remind students humans have culture because of their ability to create symbols. Ask them to name a few symbols.

3. Explain when people read, write, or draw, they use symbols.

4. We know a great deal about ancient Egypt because of the symbols they left behind. Show the slides from the kit, *A Look at Daily Life in Ancient Egypt*. While showing the slides, discuss the relevance of the symbols.

5. Next, discuss how the ancient Egyptians also used symbols for writing and reading, but the symbols they used are different than the ones used today. They had three different forms of writing used for different purposes. One form, called hieroglyphics, was used by the scribes in the temples and pyramids.

6. Use either the *Hieroglyphics Encoder* kit or make your own set of symbols to explain and demonstrate hieroglyphics and how they were written.

7. Have the students pair off and write simple messages to one another using hieroglyphics.

8. Create a bulletin board where students can leave messages for one another using hieroglyphics.

Reflection

The messages the students produce for one another and whether they are read provide assessment. Also, ask students to write a simple statement relating hieroglyphics to the big idea that culture is related to humans' ability to symbolize. Another reflective activity is to ask students to discuss how it might feel to have to learn and use different ways of writing and communicating. Some students could create a skit describing how it might feel. Ask students to record their thoughts in their journals.

Hope and Meaning

Related Big Ideas

 Every cultural trait has form, meaning, and function.

 Cultures are formed by their members to support survival and to increase quality of life.

 Culture affects the behavior of its members, and its members influence it.

 Members of cultures share basic needs: food and shelter to survive and hope and meaning in their lives. All aspects of a culture relate to these needs.

What To Do

1. Ask the class what they think *hope* is.

2. Ask students whether they have dreams and hopes and why they think it is important, or not important, for people to have dreams and hopes.

3. Explain all people and cultures have dreams and hopes because this is what gives life meaning. The ancient Egyptians also had dreams and hopes. Many of their dreams and hopes centered on what would happen to them after death. In particular, the pharaohs devoted a great deal of thought and resources to building tombs (pyramids) for their afterlife.

4. Show the video *Ancient Lives: Dreams and Rituals.*

5. Divide the class into six groups. Each group researches one of the following questions pertaining to pyramids:

   a. Why were the pyramids built?

   b. Where were the pyramids built and why were they built there?

   c. What materials were used to build the pyramids and why were these materials used?

   d. Who built the pyramids and what were their lives like?

   e. How were the pyramids built?

   f. How can the exterior and interior of the pyramids be described?

   (An alternative might be to have the students generate a list of questions they think they need to answer).

6. Allow the students to use the Internet, diagrams, and books to research the questions, and have the groups share their research with the class. Have individuals or groups brainstorm methods for building an exterior and interior model of a pyramid.

Reflection

Have the students write in their journals about what they see as their class' hopes and dreams. Later, ask students to share their reflections with the class and write a list of classroom goals and wishes.

Assessment

OBJECTIVE 1

Demonstrate an understanding of the concept *culture* and the following related components of cultural study: technology, ideology, sociology, and attitude.

EXPLANATION

Have students use the Guidelines for Research Projects (see blacklines) to guide their preparation of a project on some aspect of ancient Egypt. This becomes part of the display on ancient Egypt and school culture.

CRITERIA

Use the Research Project Scoring Rubric (see blacklines) to evaluate the project.

SECTION THREE

Forces of Change

OBJECTIVE 2

Identify evidence of cultural change and causes for change in ancient Egypt as well as in the students' classroom and school.

Imposed Change
An Outside Force

Related Big Ideas

 A culture is made up of many ways of acting and thinking. Some of these ways are changing; some are remaining the same.

 All cultures change, and many factors contribute to change.

What To Do

1. Prior to the students' arrival, rearrange the classroom furniture.

2. Explain to the students that you walked into the classroom this morning and were surprised to find that someone had changed the position of the furniture overnight. Someone introduced a change to the classroom culture.

3. Introduce big ideas numbers 7 and 8. Explain many factors contribute to change; however, just because one change has been introduced does not mean everything about classroom culture changes. Use Notes Concerning Cultural Change and Change and Culture (see blacklines).

 4. Ask the students to keep a log during the day of how the furniture rearrangement influenced change in the classroom.

 5. At the end of the day, discuss the changes and complete the Chart of Changes Due to Furniture Rearrangement (see blacklines).

SkyLight Training and Publishing Inc.

Reflection

The students' logs provide an ongoing account of the changes the students noted during the day. Encourage the students to share their ideas with one another and discuss their observations. Make sure students verbalize the ideas that all cultures change and, when change is introduced to a culture, some aspects of the culture change while others remain the same.

Ask students to use a Flow Chart (see blacklines) to do one of the following:

1. Depict factors that may cause their own family to change.

2. Note how advances in technology are changing the class, school, or community culture.

Environment and Change

Related Big Ideas

 A culture is made up of many ways of acting and thinking. Some of these ways are changing; some are remaining the same.

 All cultures change, and many factors contribute to change.

 Cultural changes are introduced through both inside and outside sources (i.e., environment, conflict, acculturation, diffusionism, or innovation).

What To Do

Note: As a prerequisite to this experience, students need to be able to describe observations and have an understanding of what environment is. Also, try to do this activity on a rainy or snowy day.

1. Review what was learned in the previous learning experience, Imposed Change: An Outside Force.

2. Use an overhead projector to show a clear dish filled with water. Ask the students to describe what they see on the screen. Next, add a drop of blue food coloring to the water and ask the students to describe what they see now. Ask what created the change. Next, add a drop of yellow food coloring and ask them to describe the change. Ask students what they think change is. After some discussion, provide a

definition of change using Notes Concerning Cultural Change (see blacklines).

3. Explain that all cultures can change, and many factors may cause changes to take place. Sometimes, changes are created by something from "outside" culture or by some force that is not part of it, such as when the water was changed by adding the drop of food coloring. Something that was not part of the water changed it. Ask students to brainstorm examples of things that are changed by something else, that is, by an outside force.

4. Explain that one outside force that can change a culture is the environment. Refer to the fact that their own classroom culture is affected by the weather. Ask students to name a few ways the weather has changed classroom routines for the day.

5. Divide the students into groups of two or three. Ask them to use a mind map to brainstorm ways their classroom culture is affected by the outside force of the weather. Use chart paper to record the mind map.

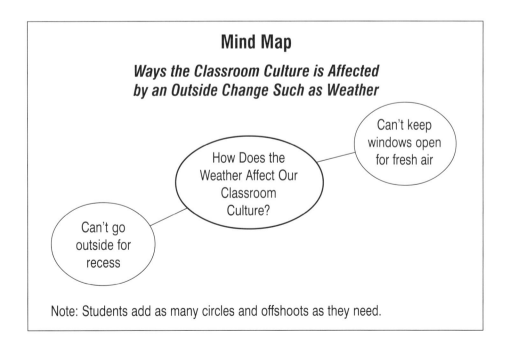

Mind Map

Ways the Classroom Culture is Affected by an Outside Change Such as Weather

How Does the Weather Affect Our Classroom Culture?

Can't keep windows open for fresh air

Can't go outside for recess

Note: Students add as many circles and offshoots as they need.

6. After students share their ideas with the class, ask them to imagine what it would be like if the weather changed so that it rained every day, permanently.

Reflection

Students write in their journals the big ideas that support this lesson: All cultures can change, and outside forces such as the environment can cause cultures to change. Listen to the discussions during the group and cooperative activities to determine whether the students have an understanding of the concept of change and outside forces that influence change. Ask students to think of other outside forces that might cause a culture to change.

Ask the students to write and prepare an essay, skit, poem, song, or dance with narration explaining how they think the environment may influence cultures today. As an alternative, ask students to write in their journal about how they think the environment may influence cultures today, and have them share their ideas with a partner.

Environment as an Influence

Related Big Ideas

 A culture is made up of many ways of acting and thinking. Some of these ways are changing; some are remaining the same.

 All cultures change, and many factors contribute to change.

 Cultural changes are introduced through both inside and outside sources (i.e., environment, conflict, acculturation, diffusionism, or innovation).

What To Do

1. Dress up as an Egyptian farmer.

2. As the farmer, tell the students you heard they have been learning about culture and change.

3. Ask students to summarize what they have learned thus far.

4. Tell the story of how the people of ancient Egypt, particularly the farmers, depended on the flooding of the Nile. (Use books on Egypt and the video *Ancient Lives: An Artist's Life* to help tell the story.) If something changed in that flood cycle, such as if the floods did not come or the floods were too high, farmers would have to change their ways.

5. Provide students with resources on agriculture and products in ancient Egypt.

6. Divide the students into cooperative groups. Ask each group to find one fact about how some aspect of the ancient Egyptian society depended on the Nile. Have students fill out the Aspects of the Nile That Influenced Egypt (see blacklines) form. Bring the groups together and list the facts as they are being shared.

7. Relate the statement that Egypt has been referred to as "the gift of the Nile." Ask students what might happen if that gift had been removed. Ask them to write their reflections in their journals.

Reflection

Ask students to write in their journals a few statements about the following:

1. What might have happened to the ancient Egyptians if the Nile suddenly no longer produced its gifts?

2. Is there anything in their local environment that is as important as the Nile?

Some students may choose to prepare a skit demonstrating how the Egyptian culture had to adapt when the Nile did not flood as it usually did.

Change Through Acculturation

Related Big Ideas

 A culture is made up of many ways of acting and thinking. Some of these ways are changing; some are remaining the same.

 All cultures change, and many factors contribute to change.

 Cultural changes are introduced through both inside and outside sources (i.e., environment, conflict, acculturation, diffusionism, or innovation).

What To Do

Note: This activity requires the cooperation of other classroom teachers; arrangements must be made in advance.

1. Review how outside forces may cause a culture to change. Remind students that some things about a culture change because of outside forces, and some do not change. Tell them outside forces other than the environment may cause a culture to change. For example, when one culture meets another culture, they may learn different ways of doing things. One may see that the other culture has a better way of doing something and may decide to try that way for themselves. This kind of change is chosen by the culture.

2. Explain sometimes one culture forces another to change. Give examples from ancient Egypt, such as when the Hyksos introduced ancient Egyptians to the use of the horse and chariot during battle.

3. Discuss forced and chosen changes and introduce the word *acculturation* in making the distinction (see Notes Concerning Cultural Change in the blacklines section).

4. Explain to students they are going to experience acculturation at work. Divide the class into groups of two to four students. Each group observes in another teacher's classroom for thirty minutes and takes notes using a Classroom Observation Form (see blacklines), which identifies a few items to help them focus their observations. The list of items to look for may change, but use the same form for each classroom observed.

5. After their observations are completed, have students use the Classroom Comparison Chart (see blacklines) to compare the different ways the classes did things.

Reflection

Carefully guide students to reflect on the ways teachers do things in their classrooms and why they may do things differently. Relate this to all cultures, including the ancient Egyptians. Ask students to answer these questions in their journals: What is acculturation? Is acculturation a good or bad thing for cultures and why?

They may share their writings with other students. As an alternative, students might prepare a skit, song, or essay that responds to the same prompt.

Change and Conflict

Related Big Ideas

 A culture is made up of many ways of acting and thinking. Some of these ways are changing; some are remaining the same.

 All cultures change, and many factors contribute to change.

 Cultural changes are introduced through both inside and outside sources (i.e., environment, conflict, acculturation, diffusionism, or innovation).

What To Do

1. Review what has been learned about forces that cause cultures to change.

2. Explain conflict from either outside or inside a culture may cause it to change. Ask students to cite examples of conflicts within the classroom that may have caused a rule to change or caused a change in how something was done.

3. Introduce an Egyptian warrior puppet. The puppet could be ready-made or could be made out of paper mâché and cloth. Have the warrior tell how several different conflicts involving other countries affected the Egyptians and eventually led to the end of ancient Egyptian civilization.

4. Show the video *Ancient Lives: The Year of the Hyena.* Discuss how conflict influenced the Egyptians.

5. Using puppets, create a scenario where a classroom conflict arises because of conflict in which others outside the classroom are involved.

6. Lead a discussion as to how the outside conflict might have caused the classroom to change its way of doing something.

Reflection

Ask students to work singly, in pairs, or in groups to prepare a skit, poem, song, or poster depicting the influence conflict can have on cultures. These can be recorded and used later for the museum display. Instruct the students to try to include the influence that conflict had on Egyptian culture.

Change and Innovation

Related Big Ideas

 A culture is made up of many ways of acting and thinking. Some of these ways are changing; some are remaining the same.

 All cultures change, and many factors contribute to change.

 Cultural changes are introduced through both inside and outside sources (i.e., environment, conflict, acculturation, diffusionism, or innovation).

What To Do

Note: This activity can be related to a science unit on machines, inventions, and the inventive spirit.

1. Dress as an Egyptologist. Explain that scientists know from the tombs of the great pharaohs that the Egyptians were the first to invent many different things people still use. Discuss the Characteristics of Borrowing and Innovation (see blacklines). Explain that students are going to go on a treasure hunt to find out about those contributions.

 2. Set up various learning stations about Egyptian contributions to farming, medicine and science, timekeeping, embalming, court systems, architecture, and so forth. Students visit at least two stations and take notes using the Learning Station Notes on Egyptian Innova-

tions form (see blacklines). (Adapt visit duration for varied group sizes and other scheduling factors.)

3. Ask students to share what they have learned. Begin an ongoing list of inventions made by the ancient Egyptians and list how such inventions have influenced society today (see Egyptian Inventions and Influence Chart in the blacklines section).

4. As the students add to the list, remind them the inventions reveal forces that changed the Egyptian culture from the inside and their inventions also became forces that influenced other cultures from the outside as other cultures began to learn from the Egyptians and borrow their ideas (diffusionism).

Reflection

Have students write essays or prepare skits, dioramas, posters, or songs explaining how Egyptian culture (as well as students' own cultures) would have been different if the Egyptians had not invented the calendar.

 SkyLight Training and Publishing Inc.

Assessment

OBJECTIVE 2

Identify evidence of cultural change and causes for change in ancient Egypt as well as in the students' classroom and school.

TEST QUESTIONS

1. Name three big ideas about the relationship between culture and change.

2. What is an inside force that causes a culture to change?

3. What is an outside force that causes a culture to change?

4. What is one thing the ancient Egyptians changed because of an outside force?

5. Name at least three things other cultures borrowed from the ancient Egyptians.

6. Explain how the environment can cause cultures to change.

7. Compare how conflict influenced change in our classroom and among the ancient Egyptians.

8. What do you think is most influential in changing cultures: inside forces or outside forces? Explain why you think that way.

9. Tell how you would use innovation to change the lighting in our classroom and to improve our classroom culture.

10. What is a practice in our classroom that other classrooms could learn about through diffusionism?

11. What change could have taken place so that Egypt would not be the"Gift of the Nile"?

12. Explain why you agree or disagree with this statement: The ancient Egyptians suddenly changed everything about their culture.

EVALUATION CRITERIA

1. A point system for correct responses.

2. Questions number 1, 8, 9, 10, 11, and 12 need to be worth more points because they require more thinking.

3. For the first question, look for answers related to big ideas numbers 7, 8, and 9.

 SkyLight Training and Publishing Inc.

SECTION FOUR

Comparing and Contrasting Cultures

OBJECTIVE 3

Apply identified cultural understanding to compare and contrast characteristics of the ancient Egyptian with students' classroom and school cultures.

Comparing Tools, Furniture, Clothing, and Foods

Related Big Ideas

 Culture helps people describe, explain, and predict behavior for individuals and groups.

 Members of cultures share basic needs: food and shelter to survive and hope and meaning in their lives. All aspects of a culture relate to these needs.

What To Do

1. Ask students to summarize what they have learned about culture and change and prepare a class list of what they now know.

2. Remind them that the big ideas (see introduction) they have been discussing can be related to all cultures, from the ancient Egyptians to their own classroom cultures.

3. Refer to big idea number 5. Point out that one of the functions of culture is that it provides a guide for behavior. This is true for people today, and it was true for the ancient Egyptians. Such guides help people predict the behavior of most individuals in that culture. Ask students if they can predict what they will be doing at lunchtime. People need food and have a routine they follow to make sure they get the food they need, at a time they need it.

4. The ancient Egyptians also had routines that involved food and nourishment. Show the video *Ancient Lives: The Valley of the Kings*.

5. Divide the students into groups of two to three and have them fill out the Compare and Contrast Chart (see blacklines). Students need to compare and contrast the ancient Egyptian culture with their own classroom or school cultures in terms of tools, furniture, clothing, utensils, and foods. They may use notes from the video and books to assist them with the task. Students might even collect artifacts of tools, furniture, clothing, utensils, and foods they use. These artifacts might be revealed during sharing time. Have the groups share their comparisons with the class.

6. Remind the students that although the cultures are different in many ways, both the ancient Egyptians and their classroom have predictable ways of doing things related to tools, furniture, clothing, utensils, and foods. Just as they would expect to find certain things in an ancient Egyptian house, they would expect to find certain things in classrooms.

Reflection

The compare and contrast activity requires the students to relate the comparison to predictable behavior. Ask students to imagine they are in an ancient Egyptian school. Which things would be the same? Which would be different? What is the basis for their predictions about these things?

For homework, have the students brainstorm family routines that allow them to make certain predictions or have certain expectations and collect artifacts of these routines. These can be shared with the class the next day.

Comparing and Contrasting Cultural Stories

Related Big Ideas

 The formation of culture depends on humans' ability to symbolize.

 Every cultural trait has form, meaning, and function.

 Cultures are formed by their members to support survival and to increase quality of life.

 Members of cultures share basic needs: food and shelter to survive and hope and meaning in their lives. All aspects of a culture relate to these needs.

What To Do

Note: This could be a controversial learning experience. Use only after determining the sensitivity of the students' families concerning religious beliefs and exposure to alternative religious ideology. Teachers may want to talk with parents first.

1. Dress as an Egyptian scribe.

2. Remind the students that cultures depend on humans' ability to symbolize. People use symbols when they read and write. They also use symbols in the stories they tell. Most of the time, ancient Egyptians told stories or myths to explain certain aspects about their world. But, stories are also created to tell people how to behave or

what they should do in certain situations. Stories improve life. Stories are an important part of all cultures.

3. Read "Isis and Osiris" from the book *The Illustrated Book of Myths: Tales and Legends of the World.*

4. Ask students to tell what the story is explaining (cultivation, good, and evil). Then, ask if they can think of any stories they have heard that explain the presence of evil, such as the story of Adam and Eve in the Bible.

5. Next, read the story "First Things" from the book in step 3. (This story explains the creation of the world.) Again, ask students to think of a similar story, such as the chapter in the Bible that explains the creation of the world.

6. Reiterate that all cultures tell stories, many of which explain certain aspects of the world.

 7. Have the students create stories, poems, or skits explaining some aspect of classroom life. The following are some examples: Why classrooms were created; How lunch boxes were invented; How pencils were invented; How homework was invented; and so forth.

Reflection

The activity of creating a myth provides the students with an opportunity for reflection. Have the students write in their journals why stories are an important part of all cultures. Ask them to make up stories, poems, or skits to describe some aspect of the world.

Comparing and Contrasting Writing Systems

Related Big Ideas

 The formation of culture depends on humans' ability to symbolize.

 Every cultural trait has form, meaning, and function.

 Cultures are formed by their members to support survival and to increase quality of life.

 Members of cultures share basic needs: food and shelter to survive and hope and meaning in their lives. All aspects of a culture relate to these needs.

What To Do

1. Ask students to summarize what they learned about hieroglyphics.

SkyLight Training and Publishing Inc.

2. If the students do not know how to prepare and use a Venn diagram, teach them. *The Cooperative Think Tank* (Bellanca 1990) is an excellent source to use for teaching students how to use a Venn diagram.

3. Have pairs of students use a Venn diagram (see blacklines) to compare and contrast hieroglyphics to their writing system. Share the comparisons with the entire group.

Reflection

Ask students to write in their journals why they think the ancient Egyptians used pictures for their writing and people today do not. Also, students might research the number system the Egyptians used and comment in their journals about their preference in number systems.

Assessment

OBJECTIVE 3

Apply identified cultural understanding to compare and contrast characteristics of the ancient Egyptian with the students' classroom or school cultures.

EXPLANATION

The research project, introduced in Introduction of Research Project in section 1, requires each student to prepare a project telling about some aspect of life in ancient Egypt. The students share their projects with the entire class. Students are required to learn from each other's projects and to take notes in their journals. At the completion of the project presentations and the activities for objective number 3, the students need to complete the Compare and Contrast Test (see blacklines).

Note: The top categories may vary according to the students' projects. Also, more categories may be added.

EVALUATION CRITERIA

Students should have at least one correct statement in each box of the Compare and Contrast Test. They receive six points for each box if they have at least one correct statement in the box. They can receive up to ten points of extra credit for additional correct statements placed in each box.

SECTION FIVE

Tools of Cultural Study

OBJECTIVE 4

Describe and apply simple procedures (observations, interviews, and archaeological digs) used by archaeologists, sociologists, and anthropologists to study cultures.

Archaeology
Should We Dig Up the Past?

Related Big Ideas

Cultural changes can be observed and recorded.

What To Do

Note: This particular learning experience will probably take two to three class periods for completion.

1. Dress as an archaeologist; wear something like a safari shirt and a safari hat.

2. Ask students to discuss why scientists know so much about ancient Egypt.

3. Ask students if they can define the terms archaeology and archaeologist.

4. After they have tried to define archaeology and archaeologist, explain the word *archaeology* comes from the Greek language and means "the study of what is ancient." Also, tell the students an archaeologist is someone who studies "the material remains of past human life and activities" (Webster 1980, 58). Thus, in archaeology, a person examines such things as fossils, relics, artifacts, and monuments.

5. Explain how things from the past are preserved and discuss the many sources archaeologists use to gain information about the past. (Note: *Eyewitness Book: Archaeology* is an excellent resource.)

6. Ask students to debate whether the past should be excavated.

Reflection

Prior to the debate, students might prepare persuasive essays that present their response to the question "Should the past be excavated?" The Hamburger Model of Persuasive Writing (Center for Gifted Education, College of William and Mary, in press) is an excellent tool for guiding students' persuasive writing endeavors (see blacklines).

After the debate, ask students to backtrack and reread their own essay and comment in their journals about one point someone persuaded them was important for deciding the question. Did it change their position? Why or why not?

Anthropologist
Nonobtrusive Observation

Related Big Ideas

Cultural changes can be observed and recorded.

What To Do

1. Ask students to define what an anthropologist is. Note differences between anthropologists and archaeologists (see the previous learning experience, Archaeology: Should We Dig Up the Past?). Explain the difference between the two: The anthropologist looks at "the distribution, origin, classification, and relationship of races, physical characteristics, environmental and social relations, and culture" (Webster 1980, 48), whereas the archaeologist examines material remains of humans.

2. Explain how anthropologists become part of a culture and spend a great deal of time observing the culture over a period of time to learn about it. To do this well, they must develop their ability to observe, particularly their ability to see and record small details.

3. Explain the concept of *nonobtrusive observers* as persons who try to become as unnoticeable as possible so they will not get in the way of how the people would normally do things. List their characteristics: (1) not interfere with conversations, (2) sit in places where they will not be noticed much, and (3) try not interact in any way with the people being observed.

4. Place students in pairs. As one of the pair observes and takes notes on some assigned aspect of school life for ten minutes, the other student in the pair observes the observer and take notes about his or her behavior as a nonobtrusive observer. Both students can use the Nonobtrusive Observation Form (see blacklines).

5. Ask pairs to share their experience with each other, the class, or another pair.

6. A variation of this learning experience: Assign a student to observe another student and keep it a secret from the person he or she is observing. At the end of the day, there could be a revealing of who was observing whom, after students try to identify who they thought was observing them.

Reflection

Ask students to write about their experience as observers: What was hard? What was easy? Was it enjoyable? Ask them about their experience in the reverse role (as the observed): How did they feel about being observed? Did they notice that they were being observed? Which role did they prefer: observed or observer? Why or why not?

Anthropologist
Effective Interviews

Related Big Ideas

 Cultural changes can be observed and recorded.

What To Do

1. Explain how anthropologists learn about aspects of various cultures by interviewing individuals.

2. Discuss the components of good interview questions and appropriate interview etiquette. Remind students that good interview questions meet these criteria:

   • They are clear and concise

   • They do not lead the person who is being interviewed to respond in a particular way

   • They are limited in number

   • They are open-ended so that there could be different kinds of responses

   • They focus on, and stick to, the topic and purpose of the interview

   • They are reviewed first by another individual to determine their clarity

 3. Have the students prepare questions, interview various individuals in the school, and report the interview results.

Reflection

Ask students to write in their journals about why it is important for anthropologists to develop good interview techniques. Ask them to note in a short paragraph in their journals what they think was their best question (in terms of getting good, full responses) and why they think the question worked so well. What about their worst question (based on the poor responses that were elicited)? How did the two differ?

Archaeology
The Dig and the Grid System

Related Big Ideas

Cultural changes can be observed and recorded.

What To Do

1. Invite an archaeologist to talk with the class. The archaeologist might demonstrate the tools used and might explain how scientists study cultures by examining artifacts left by that culture. Also, the archaeologist might demonstrate how artifacts are found through *digs* and might include a description of a grid system.

2. If possible, have the students visit an archaeological site. An alternative might be to use the video *Ancient Egypt: Digging Up Her Rich Past* with this activity.

3. Use an indoor sandbox and have the students simulate a grid system by using strings on the sandbox organized in a similar way to those used at an archaeological site. Ask students to find artifacts and record their findings in the same manner scientists would use, indicating the grids in which the artifacts were found.

Reflection

Ask students to compare an archaeological dig to a treasure hunt and write about it in their journals.

SkyLight Training and Publishing Inc.

Anthropology and Archaeology
Time Capsule

Related Big Ideas

Cultural changes can be observed and recorded.

What To Do

1. After reviewing archaeology and anthropology, explain the students are going to prepare a time capsule that tells about their classroom culture.

2. Give each student a Time Capsule Worksheet (see blacklines) to help them plan what to put in the time capsule and why each item is to be included.

3. After the students have individually planned a time capsule, have them share their ideas with the class.

4. Then, develop criteria for selecting those items that will actually go into the time capsule for the class.

5. This time capsule might be part of the students' final display.

Reflection

The worksheet gives the class an opportunity for reflection. Ask students to imagine they were opening a time capsule from a different classroom. Would the items be similar or different? Why do they think this?

Assessment

OBJECTIVE 4

Describe and apply simple procedures (observations, interviews, and archaeological digs) used by archaeologists, sociologists, and anthropologists to study cultures.

BUILDING A PORTFOLIO

This assessment consists of compiling a portfolio. Students may handwrite, type, illustrate, color, or embellish items to reflect their personality. Suggest the following items:

Item 1. Write an essay, song, or poem describing why it is important to preserve the past. Make sure you are persuasive.

Item 2. Draw a diagram of a grid system an archaeologist would use. Include in your diagram drawings of at least three artifacts that might have been found in excavations of ancient Egypt. Below the grid, list the names of the artifacts and the grid numbering of their location. On a separate piece of paper, write a paragraph describing the considerations for preparing a quality grid.

Item 3. Think about what you have learned about interview questions. Pretend you are an anthropologist who is studying

the culture of the modern United States. One way that you have decided to study this culture is by looking at the songs that have been written. You choose a famous musician to interview. Develop the interview questions you would ask this musician about what influenced him or her to write one particular song he or she is famous for. Remember you want to know what this musician and song is saying about modern society in the United States. Record your interview questions. Be sure to identify the musician and the famous song.

Item 4. Think about what we have learned about being a non-obtrusive observer. Design a newspaper ad requesting applications for a nonobtrusive observer. This newspaper ad should describe the job, give the job requirements, and mention the job compensation. Write the ad in the form you would see it in the newspaper.

Item 5. Reflect on whether you would rather be an anthropologist or an archaeologist. Write about which you would rather be and why. Remember, your reflections need to reveal the differences between an anthropologist and an archaeologist.

CRITERIA

Use the Tools for Cultural Study Portfolio Scoring Rubric (see blacklines).

SECTION SIX

Creating a
Museum Display

OBJECTIVE 5

Demonstrate an understanding of the occupations, practices, and routines associated with museums as preparation for a comparative display on culture and change in ancient Egypt and in the students' classroom.

Occupations, Practices, and Routines of Museums

Related Big Ideas

 Cultural changes can be observed and recorded.

What To Do

Note: This activity could follow the second learning experience, Funding of Museums.

1. Have the director of a museum talk with the class about the occupations, practices, and routines of museums.

2. Have students draw mind maps of the implications for the display they must prepare.

Reflection

Have students prepare essays about why museums are important. Ask them to predict the audience for their displays. Who do they want to see it? Will their audience influence their displays? In what way? Evaluate the essay using the Scoring Rubric for Essay on Importance of Museums (see blacklines).

Funding of Museums

Related Big Ideas

 Cultural changes can be observed and recorded.

What To Do

Note: This learning experience needs two class periods that are held a week apart from one another.

1. Ask students to brainstorm what they think are the various expenditures that go into running a museum. Write their responses on chart paper.

2. Next, ask how they think museums are funded.

3. Tell the students they are going on a scavenger hunt to find out how museums are funded.

4. Brainstorm the various ways students can obtain information about how museums are funded.

5. For homework, each student finds one tidbit of information about the funding of museums. They have one week in which to find their tidbit, which they will share with the class.

6. Have students write their tidbit and its source on a 3" x 5" index card and encourage them to decorate their cards to reflect the tidbit they found.

 7. For the second class session, develop a class collage that includes all the tidbit index cards. Students share their tidbit with the class and then arrange it on the collage.

Reflection

As a follow-up, each student estimates how much he or she thinks it costs to run a local museum. These estimates are written on a piece of paper with the student's name on it. Then, a group of students may write to a museum to obtain an operating budget to share with the class. The class can determine who was closest in his or her estimate and how he or she came up with that estimate.

Visit to a Museum

Related Big Ideas

Cultural changes can be observed and recorded.

What To Do

1. Visit a museum.

2. Take notes on display techniques using the Worksheet for Museum Visit (see blacklines). Suggest to students they use at least five displays they liked and at least two they did not like in their notetaking.

Reflection

Ask students to draw a map of the museum and mark the exhibits that they would go to again, and tell why. Using their worksheets, ask them to compile a list of things about the displays they liked, and a list of things they didn't like.

Making a Display

Related Big Ideas

 Cultural changes can be observed and recorded.

What To Do

 1. Students plan and prepare a display that compares and contrasts ancient Egyptian and classroom cultures and demonstrates an understanding of the relationship between the concepts of culture and change.

2. Place the display in a public place, such as a museum or a library.

Reflection

Ask students to write about the pluses, minuses, and interesting questions or information that evolved during this unit of study and have them develop a newscast about the pluses, minuses, and interesting information.

Assessment

OBJECTIVE 5

Demonstrate an understanding of the occupations, practices, and routines associated with museums as preparation for a comparative display on culture and change in ancient Egypt and in the students' classroom.

EXPLANATION

Have a museum director critique components of the students' display:

- Quality of information about the concept *culture*
- Quality of information about the forces of cultural change
- Quality of information about life in ancient Egypt
- Quality of information about class culture
- Quality of comparisons
- Aesthetic qualities of the display

EVALUATION CRITERIA

Use the Rubric for Museum Display Assessment (see blacklines) to evaluate.

Blacklines

Blacklines Contents

Rubrics

The Problem Statement

You are the director of a children's museum in Memphis, Tennessee, and have been charged with the responsibility of preparing a special display celebrating the city's 200th year of existence. Memphis was named after an ancient Egyptian capital and the exhibit is to include a comparison of the ancient Egyptian culture and the culture at one elementary school in the city—Opportunity Elementary. You expect thousands of children will visit the museum to see this display. You want them to leave your museum with a clear understanding of how culture relates to the past and the present. You have heard from reliable sources that the city council is considering the reduction of funding to the museum. The museum already has received federal funding cuts. If the city also reduces its funding, the museum will have to close. This increases the pressure for you to provide a quality display with limited funds.

The Knowledge Status Chart

Know?	Need-to-Know?	Find Out?

Chart for Comparing Definitions

My definition for culture was _____

_____

_____

_____

The definition given to my class was _____

_____

_____

_____

How are these definitions alike?	How are these definitions different?

Team Findings

Date: _____

Team Members: _____

Examples of Classroom Technology	Examples of Classroom Ideology
Examples of Classroom Sociology	Examples of Classroom Attitude

Guidelines for Research Projects

Student's Name: _____

Possible Topic(s) of Interest: _____

Project Due Date: _____

1. Choose a topic that interests you.

2. Use a minimum of three resources to research this topic. These resources can be the Internet, books (only one encyclopedia), tapes, videos, museums, interviews of experts, and other sources.

3. Your report may be either typed or written in neat handwriting.

4. Describe what life was like in ancient Egypt (pertaining to your topic).

5. Write one paragraph comparing your ancient Egypt topic to current life in your community or (if appropriate) classroom. Remember that a comparison includes a description of likenesses and differences.

6. Give a visual or auditory presentation of your topic.

7. Remember, your classmates will depend on the information presented in your report, so make sure that the information is accurate and complete without being too lengthy. Be prepared to present your project to the class on the date shown above.

8. Also, remember that your project will be used as part of a display on ancient Egypt, so aim for museum quality!

NOTES AND QUESTIONS: (Use this space for notes or questions as you begin your project.)

Notes Concerning Cultural Change

Schools of Thought   Most theories of cultural change are related to four schools of thought.

Evolutionism   All societies pass through a predetermined continuum of development because humans share the same mental processes. Woods labeled this the "psychic unit of mankind" (1975, 2).

Diffusionism   Humans are not particularly inventive. Change comes to cultures due to "grand scale borrowing" (Woods 1975, 3). Diffusionists assert certain cultures developed under favorable conditions and then spread to other parts of the world. There are different schools of diffusionism:

Pan Egyptian School: According to this school, the favorable circumstances needed for developing a culture occurred only once—in ancient Egypt. After this culture developed, it spread to the rest of the world.

Culture Circle School: Proponents claim different culture centers developed independently and then spread to different parts of the world. These anthropologists maintain that (1) culture centers were few in number, (2) human culture resulted from the diffusion of single traits together with the migration of people with whole complexes of traits from the centers, and (3) diffusion radiated outward from the centers and can be traced back to them by description and comparison of culture traits (Hugill and Dickson 1988).

American School: Proponents agree with the culture circle school. They propose (1) the most dense clustering occurs at the center of the culture area, where the ecological conditions are the most favorable, (2) the most favorable ecological niche is at the center of the culture, which is identified by the elaboration and dominance of cultural patterns, and (3) those patterns furthest from the center were the oldest and were diffused earlier than those that were closer (Woods 1975).

Acculturation   This is a special kind of diffusion that occurs when two previously independent cultural traditions come into continuous contact, with enough intensity to foster extensive changes in one or both cultures (Woods 1975). *Acculturation* is "the reciprocal modulations that occur when individuals from two or more different sociocultural systems come into contact" (Spindler 1977, 31).

Neorevolutionism   Proponents espouse culturology—culture evolves according to its own laws—as similar to the concept of evolution in animals (Woods 1975).

Change and Culture

Change

Smith (1976) defined *change* as "a succession of events which produce over time a modification or replacement of particular patterns or units by other novel ones" (13). Smith delineated these qualities of change:

1. Change always involves an alteration of some pattern or thing.

2. Change is always temporal as well as spatial.

3. Change is infeasible without movement.

4. Change always involves some reference to events which mark a transition.

5. Change is always change of patterns and units in a particular space and time.

Culture Change

Spindler and Spindler (1959) specifically defined culture change as "any modification in the way of life of a people, whether consequent to internal developments or to contact between two peoples with unlike ways of life" (37).

Chart of Changes
Due to Furniture Rearrangement

When the furniture was moved, these things **REMAINED THE SAME** in our classroom	When the furniture was moved, these things **CHANGED** in our classroom

Flow Chart

Problem:

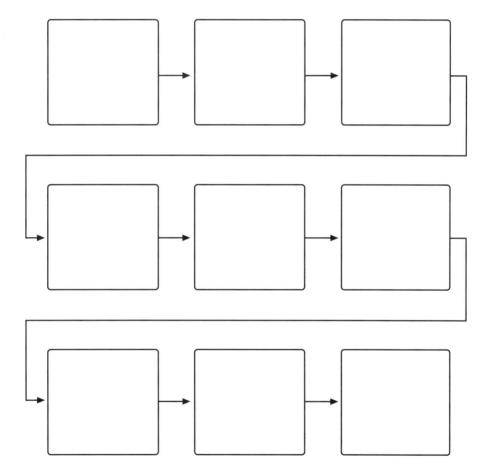

Adapted with permission from *Patterns for Thinking, Patterns for Transfer,* by Robin Fogarty and James Bellanca, IRI/Skylight Publishing Inc., 1993.

Aspects of the Nile That Influenced Egypt

Students: _____

Date: _____

We used the following source(s):

We found out the following about how the ancient Egyptian culture depended on the Nile River:

We were surprised to find . . .

Classroom Observation Form

Students: _____   Date: _____

Classroom Observed: _____

Please observe in a classroom and answer the following questions:

1. What kind of rules does the class have? (How are they alike and different from our rules?)

2. How does the class store supplies? (How is this alike and different from the way our class stores supplies?)

3. Does the class turn in and give back papers that need grading? (How is this alike and different from the way our class does this?)

Classroom Comparison Chart

		Classroom Rules	Storage	Paper Roundup
Classroom A	Alike			
	Different			
Classroom B	Alike			
	Different			
Classroom C	Alike			
	Different			
Classroom D	Alike			
	Different			

Characteristics of Borrowing and Innovation

Borrowing

- Borrowing is selective

- The extent of borrowing depends on the duration and intensity of contact between two groups

- Borrowing is more unlikely in a well-integrated culture

- Diffusion is greater among groups with similar cultural inventories

- Diffusion is usually a two-way adoption process

- Dynamics exist in the diffusion process; single traits are seldom adopted

- Traits seldom are transferred in their original configuration

- Some parts of the culture resist change more than others, and the form of resistance varies from culture to culture

Innovation

- Innovation is considered by many to be the basic source of culture change (Spindler 1977)

- Innovation is "any thought, behavior, or thing that is new because qualitatively different from existing forms . . . every innovation is an idea or constellation of ideas; but some innovations by their nature must remain mental organization only, whereas others may be given overt and tangible expression" (Barnett 1953, 7)

- All innovations can be classified according to these four basic variations: long-term variation, discovery, invention, and diffusion or borrowing (Woods 1975)

Learning Station Notes
on Egyptian Innovations

Student: _____   Date: _____

Note: Each student must choose TWO learning stations and take notes about Egyptian inventions.

1. Title of learning station: _____

   A. Inventions:

   B. How have the inventions affected the way I live today?

2. Title of learning station: _____

   A. Inventions:

   B. How have the inventions affected the way I live today?

Egyptian Inventions and Influence Chart

Egyptians' Inventions	Their Influence on Us

Compare and Contrast Chart

	The Ancient Egyptians	Our Classroom
Furniture		
Tools		
Clothing		
Utensils		
Foods		

Venn Diagram

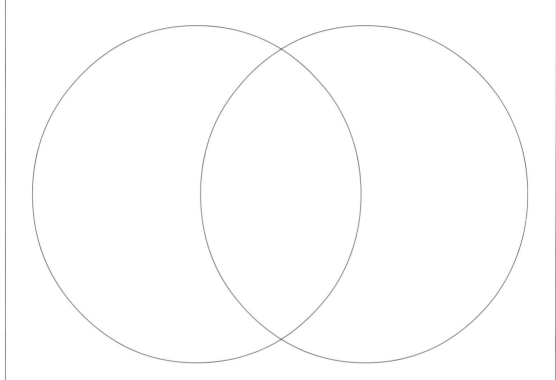

Reprinted with permission from *The Cooperative Think Tank,* by James Bellanca, IRI/SkyLight Training and Publishing, 1990.

Compare and Contrast Test

	Education	Clothing	Food	Tools	Writing
The Egyptians did this:					
We are alike because:					
We are different because:					

© SkyLight Training and Publishing Inc.

The Hamburger Model
for Persuasive Writing

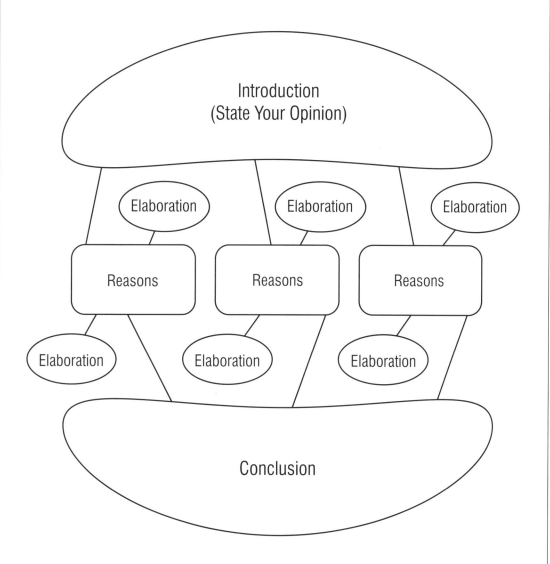

Reprinted with permission from the Center for Gifted Education, College of William and Mary, *Autobiographies,* Dubuque, IA: Kendall Hunt, in press.

Nonobtrusive Observation Form

Student who is observing: _____

Person being observed: _____

Time: _____   Date: _____

Describe the clothing the person has on.	
Describe where the person is.	
Describe what the person is doing.	

Time Capsule Worksheet

Student: _____

What would you put in a time capsule so that people in the future could learn about our class? Choose ten things that you would put in the time capsule and tell why you chose these items.

Item #1: _____ *I chose this item because . . .*	Item #2: _____ *I chose this item because . . .*
Item #3: _____ *I chose this item because . . .*	Item #4: _____ *I chose this item because . . .*
Item #5: _____ *I chose this item because . . .*	Item #6: _____ *I chose this item because . . .*
Item #7: _____ *I chose this item because . . .*	Item #8: _____ *I chose this item because . . .*
Item #9: _____ *I chose this item because . . .*	Item #10: _____ *I chose this item because . . .*

Worksheet for Museum Visit

Student: _____

Museum: _____

Date of Visit: _____

1. What is in the display?

2. How is the display organized?

3. What do you like about how the display looks?

4. What do you NOT like about how the display looks?

5. What is something that you would like to try for our display?

Journal Scoring Rubric

Student: _____

☐ Self-Evaluation ☐ Peer Evaluation ☐ Teacher Evaluation

Criteria	1 Poor	2 Below Average	3 Good	4 Outstanding
Completion of reflections	More than one reflection is missing or incomplete.	One reflection is missing or incomplete.	All reflections are completed.	All reflections and additional reflections have been included.
Mastery of concepts and big ideas	Reflections demonstrate mastery of *few* concepts presented and *many* reflections do not relate to the appropriate big idea(s).	Reflections demonstrate mastery of *most* concepts presented and *some* reflections do not relate to the appropriate big idea(s).	Reflections demonstrate mastery of *all* concepts presented and relates *all* reflections to the appropriate big idea(s).	Reflections demonstrate mastery of *all* concepts presented and relates *all* reflections to the appropriate big idea(s) in an in-depth manner.
Quality of journal presentation (cover, neatness, layout, etc.)	The presentation of the journal detracts from the reader's ability to comprehend the contents. Errors are so numerous it is difficult to read.	Key reflections are missing. Reflections meet minimum standards for neatness.	Reflections are neat and presentation contributes to the reader's content comprehension.	Key elements demonstrate neatness, creativity, and style.
Overall quality of reflections	The majority of reflections are descriptions of the activity and do not include student's insights.	Many reflections are descriptive of the activity and do not include student's insight.	Most reflections include student's insights; description is used only to link to the actual learning experience.	All reflections are in-depth and provide evidence of insight and thoughtfulness.

Scoring Rubric for Cultural Symbols Essay

Student: _____

Date: _____

Title of Essay: _____

☐ Self-Evaluation   ☐ Peer Evaluation   ☐ Teacher Evaluation

Criteria	1 Poor	2 Below Average	3 Good	4 Outstanding
Explanation of symbol	The explanation of the symbol is missing or incomplete.	The explanation of the symbol is limited.	The explanation of the symbol is clear and complete.	Provides extensive explanation of the symbol. The reader has a clear picture of what the symbol depicts.
Creativity	The symbol is a copy of another symbol and there is little or no elaboration.	The symbol and explanation are similar to other symbols and explanations.	The symbol and explanation reflect some originality and elaboration.	The symbol and explanation reflect a high degree of originality and elaboration. Both reflect great insight. The symbol is unique.
Organization	The essay does not include an introductory paragraph, explanatory paragraphs, and conclusion. Paragraphs are not organized around a central idea. The essay does not present a unified and coherent whole.	The essay includes an introductory and concluding paragraph. Supporting paragraphs are not organized around a central idea. The essay does not present a unified and coherent message.	The essay includes an introductory and concluding paragraph. All but one paragraph is organized around a central idea. The essay presents a unified and coherent message.	The essay includes well-formulated introductory and explanatory paragraphs that flow from one another. All paragraphs are organized around a central idea. The essay presents a unified and coherent message.

Usage of words	Inappropriate verb tense is used more than once. Numerous inappropriate words are used. Words that are used are redundant and essay is either not passionate or is inappropriately passionate.	Inappropriate verb tense is used one time. An inappropriate word is used once. Words that are used are redundant and essay is either not passionate or is inappropriately passionate.	Appropriate verb tense is used at all times. Appropriate words are used at all times. Language that is used is not particularly rich with imagery but is appropriate.	Appropriate verb tense is used at all times. Appropriate words are used at all times. Language that is used is rich with imagery and is passionate.
Punctuation and spelling	There are more than two punctuation and spelling errors.	There are two punctuation and spelling errors.	There is one punctuation or spelling error.	There are no punctuation or spelling errors.

Comments:

Research Project Scoring Rubric

Student: _____

☐ Self-Evaluation ☐ Peer Evaluation ☐ Teacher Evaluation

Criteria	1 Poor	2 Below Average	3 Good	4 Outstanding	Weight of Points	Total
Use of resources	Uses 0–2 sources all of the same type (i.e., encyclopedias).	Uses 3 sources of the same type (i.e., encyclopedias).	Uses a minimum of 4 sources of various types.	Uses more than 4 types of sources. At least 1 source is technology based.	x 2	
Descriptive information	Descriptive information of both cultures is missing or incomplete.	Descriptive information of both cultures is very limited. Reader must fill in the gaps.	The descriptive information meets the requirements of the project.	Provides extensive descriptive information of both cultures. The reader has a clear picture of what this aspect of life was and is like.	x 4	
Comparison of cultures	Little comparison is made between the two cultures.	Comparison is provided but is not completely one-on-one. In one instance, only one culture is described.	One-on-one comparison is made throughout the project.	Extensive comparison is provided throughout the project. Comparisons are one-on-one and reflect a high degree of analysis.	x 4	
Organization	More than one requirement is missing. Presentation detracts from reader's comprehension of its contents.	No more than one requirement is missing or incomplete. Elements meet minimum standards for neatness.	All requirements are completed according to directions. Key elements are neat and contribute to comprehension.	All entries completed and effectively organized. Key elements demonstrate neatness, creativity, and style.	x 2	

Usage	Inappropriate verb tense is used more than once. Numerous inappropriate words are used. Redundant words are used.	Inappropriate verb tense is used one time. Inappropriate words are used at least once. Redundant words are used.	Appropriate verb tense is used at all times. Appropriate words are used at all times. Language used is not particularly rich with imagery.	Appropriate verb tense is used at all times. Appropriate words are used at all times. Language used is rich with imagery.	x 2
Punctuation/ spelling	There are more than two punctuation and spelling errors.	There are two punctuation and spelling errors.	There is one punctuation or spelling error.	There are no punctuation or spelling errors.	x 2
Visual presentations*	Only one visual aid is provided, which has little visual appeal and minimal relation to the topic.	Minimal visual aids with little visual appeal and minimal relation to the topic are provided.	Visuals are colorful, capture attention, and relate specifically to the topic.	Creative visuals are provided that enhance the project. At least one is three dimensional. Visuals relate to and reinforce the topic.	x 2
Presentation of project to class*	Topic needs more explanation. Talk is hard to understand or cannot be heard. Little eye contact. Visual aids are poor. Organization is lacking.	Topic is addressed adequately. Talk volume is erratic. Notes are read. Visual aid does not enhance talk. Talk gets off track in places. Organization is lacking.	Topic is addressed adequately. Appropriate volume is used. Eye contact is intermittent. Visual aid helps presentation. Organization is good.	Topic is addressed clearly. Talk is loud enough to understand. Good eye contact. Visual aid is used effectively. Talk is well organized.	x 2
Total					

* Adapted with permission from *How to Access Authentic Learning: Training Manual*, by Kay Burke, 1993, Arlington Heights, Ill.: SkyLight Training and Publishing.

Tools of Cultural Study Portfolio Scoring Rubric

Student: _____

Date: _____

Title of Essay: _____

☐ Self-Evaluation   ☐ Peer Evaluation   ☐ Teacher Evaluation

Criteria	1 Does Not Meet Expectations	2 Meets Expectations	3 Exceeds Expectations	Weight of Points	Total
Organization	No more than one portfolio item is missing or incomplete.	All portfolio items are included and completed according to directions.	All entries are completed and effectively organized.	x 2	
Aesthetics	Items meet minimum standards for neatness. Little attention given to style and color.	Portfolio items are neat and contribute to readability and comprehension. Presentation is colorful.	Portfolio items are neat. Presentation is colorful, creative, and stylish.	x 2	
Word usage, punctuation, and spelling	Entries contain several written or proofreading errors.	Entries are error-free.	Portfolio entries reflect high level of usage and writing skills.	x 1	
Quality of reflection	One required reflection is missing.	Only those items that required reflections included a reflective piece.	All portfolio items demonstrate an advanced degree of analysis and in-depth reflection.	x 5	

© SkyLight Training and Publishing Inc.

Evidence of understanding of tools of cultural study	Demonstrates a complete understanding of less than four of the following: Why it is important to preserve the past. How to develop and use a grid system. Effective interview questions. The qualities of a nonobtrusive observer. The difference between an anthropologist and archaeologist.	Demonstrates a complete understanding of four of the following: Why it is important to preserve the past. How to develop and use a grid system. Effective interview questions. The qualities of a nonobtrusive observer. The difference between an anthropologist and archaeologist.	Demonstrates a complete understanding of all of the following: Why it is important to preserve the past. How to develop and use a grid system. Effective interview questions. The qualities of a nonobtrusive observer. The difference between an anthropologist and archaeologist.	x 5
TOTAL				

Comments:

Scoring Rubric for Essay on Importance of Museums

Student: _____

Date: _____

Title of Essay: _____

☐ Self-Evaluation   ☐ Peer Evaluation   ☐ Teacher Evaluation

Criteria	1 Poor	2 Below Average	3 Good	4 Outstanding
Persuasiveness of writing	Provides less than two reasons why museums are important or reasons that are given are not valid.	States two valid reasons why museums are important.	States three valid reasons why museums are important.	States more than three valid reasons why museums are important.
Supportive statements	Does not elaborate on reasons why museums are important. Either no clear argument is revealed or argument is not convincing.	Provides only one elaborative statement for each reason given pertaining to the importance of museums. Argument is not convincing.	Provides two elaborative statements for each reason given pertaining to the importance of museums. Argument is convincing.	Provides extensive elaboration as to why museums are important by providing more than two elaborative statements per reason. Argument is very convincing.
Organization	The essay does not include an introductory paragraph, explanatory paragraphs, and conclusion. Paragraphs are not organized around a central idea. The essay does not present a unified and coherent message.	The essay includes an introductory and concluding paragraph. Supporting paragraphs are not organized around a central idea. The essay does not present a unified and	The essay includes an introductory and concluding paragraph. All but one paragraph is organized around a central idea. The essay presents a unified and coherent message.	The essay includes well-formulated introductory and explanatory paragraphs that flow from one to another. All paragraphs are organized around a central idea. The essay presents a unified and coherent message.

Usage of words	Inappropriate verb tense is used more than once. Numerous inappropriate words are used. Words that are used are redundant, and essay is either not passionate or is inappropriately passionate.	coherent message. Inappropriate verb tense is used one time. Inappropriate words are used once. Words that are used are redundant, and essay is either not passionate or is inappropriately passionate.	Appropriate verb tense is used at all times. Appropriate words are used at all times. Language that is used is not particularly rich with imagery but is appropriate.	Appropriate verb tense is used at all times. Appropriate words are used at all times. Language that is used is rich with imagery and is passionate.
Punctuation and spelling	There are more than two punctuation and spelling errors.	There are two punctuation and spelling errors.	There is one punctuation or spelling error.	There are no punctuation or spelling errors.

Comments:

Rubric for Museum Display Assessment

(To Be Used by a Museum Staff Member)

Class: _____

School: _____

☐ Self-Evaluation   ☐ Peer Evaluation   ☐ Teacher Evaluation

Criteria	1 Weak	2 Satisfactory	3 Good
Quality of information about the concept *culture*	Information is missing about the concept *culture*. Several aspects of culture are missing.	Information about the concept *culture* is sufficient. All important aspects of culture are included.	Information about the concept *culture* is extensive. The information reveals advanced insight and understanding of the various aspects of culture and how culture is studied.
Quality of information about the forces of cultural change	Information is missing about forces of cultural change. Several forces of cultural change are missing or information about some forces is incomplete.	Information about the forces of cultural change is sufficient. All important forces of cultural change are included.	Information about the forces of cultural change is extensive. The information reveals advanced insight and understanding of the various forces of cultural change.
Quality of information about life in ancient Egypt	Information is missing about life in ancient Egypt. Several aspects of ancient Egyptian life are missing.	Information about ancient Egypt is sufficient. All important aspects of ancient Egyptian life are included.	Information about ancient Egyptian life is extensive. The information reveals advanced insight and understanding of the various aspects of ancient Egyptian life and the contributions these ancient people have made to our lives.

© SkyLight Training and Publishing Inc.

Criteria			
Quality of information about class and school culture	Information is missing about the class and school culture. Several aspects of class/school culture are missing.	Information about the class and school culture is sufficient. All important aspects of class and school culture are included.	Information about the class and school culture is extensive. The information reveals advanced insight and understanding of the various aspects of class and school culture.
Quality of comparisons	Little comparison is made between the ancient Egyptian culture and the school and classroom culture.	Comparison is provided throughout the display so that the comparison is one-to-one.	Extensive comparison is provided throughout the display. Comparison is one-on-one. Comparisons reflect a high degree of analysis.
Aesthetic qualities of the display	Minimal visuals are provided. There is little visual appeal and minimal relationship to the topic. Organization is lacking.	Visual aids are colorful, capture attention, and relate specifically to the topic. Good organization.	Creative visuals are used that reflect many characteristics of museum displays. Some displays are 3-D. All visuals reinforce the information. Well organized.

Comments:

APPENDIX A

Resources

Books

Caselli, G. 1991. *An Egyptian craftsman.* New York: Simon & Schuster.

Coote, R. 1993. *Look into the past: The Egyptians.* New York: Thomson Learning.

David, R. 1994. *Growing up in ancient Egypt.* Mahwah, NJ: Troll Associates.

David, R., and A. E. David. 1984. *History as evidence: Ancient Egypt.* New York: Warwick Press.

Donnelly, J. 1988. *Tut's mummy: Lost . . . and found.* New York: Random House.

Eschle, L. 1994. *Exploring the unknown: The curse of Tutankhamun.* San Diego, CA: Lucent Books.

Fairservis, W. A. 1963. *Egypt, gift of the Nile.* New York: Macmillan.

Hart, G. 1989. *Exploring the past: Ancient Egypt.* Orlando, FL: Harcourt Brace Jovanovich.

Haslam, A., and A. Parsons. 1995. *Make it work! Ancient Egypt.* New York: Thomson Learning.

The illustrated book of myths: Tales and legends of the world. 1995. New York: Dorling Kindersley.

Langley, A. 1986. *Life and times: Cleopatra and the Egyptians.* New York: Bookwright Press.

McIntosh, J. 1994. *Eyewitness books: Archeology.* New York: Alfred A. Knopf.

Millard, A. 1987. *Great civilizations: Egypt 3118 BC–AD 642.* New York: Franklin Watts.

———. 1995. *Mysteries of the pyramids.* Brookfield, CT: Copper Beech Books.

Miquel, P. 1979. *Ancient Egyptians.* Morristown, NJ: Silver Burdett.

Mitchell, B. 1941. *Pyramids: Great mysteries, opposing viewpoints.* San Diego, CA: Greenhaven Press.

Moreley, J., M. Bergin, and J. James. 1991. *Inside story: An Egyptian pyramid.* New York: Peter Bedrick Books.

Odijk, P. 1989. *The ancient world: The Egyptians.* Morristown, NJ: Silver Burdett Press.

Pace, M. M. 1974. *Wrapped for eternity: The story of the Egyptian mummy.* New York: McGraw-Hill.

Perl, L. 1987. *Mummies, tombs, and treasure.* New York: Clarion Books.

Purdy, S., and C. R. Sandak. 1982. *A civilization project book: Ancient Egypt.* New York: Franklin Watts.

Reeves, N. 1992. *Into the mummy's tomb.* New York: Scholastic.

Swineburne, I., and L. Swineburne. 1977. *Behind the sealed door: The discovery of the tomb and treasures of Tutankhamun.* New York: Sniffen Court Books.

Terzi, M. 1988. *The world heritage: The land of the pharaohs.* Chicago: The Children's Press.

Unstead, R. J. 1986. *See inside an Egyptian town.* New York: Warwick Press.

Ventura, P., and G. P. Ceserani. 1985. *In search of Tutankhamen.* Morristown, NJ: Silver Burdett.

Watts, F. 1992. *Egyptians.* New York: Franklin Watts.

Kits

Sibbett, E. 1978. *Ancient Egyptian Design Coloring Book.* New York: Dover Publications.

The art of stenciling: Hieroglyphic alphabet stencil. Bridgeport, CT: W. J. Fantasy.

The hieroglyphic encoder. The Straight Edge.

Weatherill, S., and S. Weatherill. 1995. *Hieroglyph it!* Hauppauge, NY: Barron's Educational Series.

The treasure chests: Ancient Egypt. London: Quarto Children's Books.

Videos and Slides

Slides

A Look at Daily Life in Ancient Egypt. 1992. Richmond, VA: Virginia Museum of Fine Arts.

Pyramid. 1988. Alexandria, VA: PBS Video.

Videos and Films

Ancient Egypt: Digging Up Her Rich Past. 1971. 51 min. film. Alexandria, VA: Time-Life Distributors.

Ancient Lives. 1986. 208 min. (8 videocassettes). Princeton, NJ: Films for the Humanities and Sciences.

> *Ancient Lives: The Village of the Craftsmen*
>
> *Ancient Lives: The Valley of the Kings*
>
> *Ancient Lives: An Artist's Life*
>
> *Ancient Lives: Temple Priests and Civil Servants*
>
> *Ancient Lives: Woman's Place*
>
> *Ancient Lives: Dreams and Rituals*
>
> *Ancient Lives: The Year of the Hyena*
>
> *Ancient Lives: The Deserted Village*

Legacy: Origins of Civilization. Vol. 3: Ancient Egypt: Land of the God Kings. 1991. 60 min. videocassette. New York: Ambrose Video Publishing.

The Lost Tomb of the Sons of Ramses II. 1993. 15 min. videocassette. Derry, NH: Chip Taylor.

APPENDIX B

Supporting Notes

3,000 Years of History Before Jesus Christ*
Around 3000 B.C., Unification of Egypt

Old Kingdom (2800–2300 B.C.)

- The capital was Memphis
- The pharaohs had gigantic tombs built for themselves—the pyramids.

Middle Kingdom (2050–1650 B.C.)

After a period of unrest:

- Thebes was the new capital.
- Expeditions left for the south.
- The Hyksos invaded the delta from the north.

New Kingdom (1550–1100 B.C.)

- The pharaohs extended the empire north and south. Some of the most famous rulers were Ramses II, Amenophis IV, and his wife, Nefertiti.
- The famous monuments of Luxor and Karnok as well as the treasure-filled tombs, such as that of Tutankhamun, were built.
- Egypt became dominated successively by the Persians, Greeks, and Romans. The population of Egypt during the reign of Amenophis III of the New Kingdom is estimated at 9 or 10 million inhabitants.

* Excerpt from P. Miquel, *Ancient Egyptians* (Morristown, N.J.: Silver Burdett, 1979), 4.

SkyLight Training and Publishing Inc.

Resource Notes
for Ancient Egypt Study

Agriculture

- The Nile produces fertile mud after floods.
- Herodotus called Egypt the "gift of the Nile."
- Area had little rainfall, so crop growing depended on the Nile floods.
- Papyrus grew in abundance in the marshes of the Nile delta. Its sprouts were eaten in salads; its pith was made into paper; its bark was woven into cords, baskets, nets, loincloths, and sandals; its stalks were fashioned into small, light boats; in bundles, it served as buoys; dried, it was used as fuel.
- Wood was so rare that plants and dried cow dung were used as fuel.

Architecture

- Obelisks are tall stones cut from a single block of granite. They often were placed in pairs in front of temples. The names of the rulers who had ordered them made were engraved in hieroglyphics on their surfaces.

Burials

- Because of Egyptian beliefs about death, burials have supplied scientists with information about ancient Egypt.
- Bodies of the rich were preserved as mummies.
- Egyptians believed that the dead needed their possessions to use in the next life.
- Boats brought the body along the river to the pyramid—coffin, clothing, furniture, food, and possessions to be buried with king.
- Body went from river to valley building where it was mummified and religious rites prepared, then moved by causeway to mortuary temple for funeral rites.
- Priests said magical rites for king to join the sun god Re in the sky.
- Boat left outside the pyramid for king to use to sail around the sky.

- Noblemen were buried in tombs, sometimes called "mastaba-tombs."
- In Old Kingdom, only the king was thought to have an afterlife; but, from Middle Kingdom onward, all people were believed to go on living after death.
- Afterlife was according to their wealth and status. Kings went to Field of Reeds in Osiris kingdom but the wealthy hoped to spend time in their tomb, their "house of eternity." Tombs had replicas of servants and scenes on their walls that depicted favorite occupations and pastimes in life.
- Food and drink were provided. At first families, then priests, then menu painted on wall.

Children

- Small children lived with their mother and other female relatives in a special part of the house.
- When sons turned 4 years old, fathers began to train them in their own profession or trade.
- Most girls married and looked after the house and their children.
- Egyptians loved their children but many died at birth or when young.
- Parents tried to prevent accidents and illness by spells and charms.
- Statues show children as important people in the family group.
- Toys were balls, tops, dolls with real hair fixed into holes, and a board game that resembled checkers. (Some toys were buried with children so they could play with them in the next world.)

Clothing

- Dress was simple because the climate was hot and dry.
- People wore jewelry made of pottery or stone, sometimes gold, silver, or copper.
- Rich people covered their heads as protection against the sun, with wigs made of real hair or grass.

Cities, Towns, and Villages

- Living areas were built around the banks of the Nile.
- Towns sprang up near pyramids during construction.

SkyLight Training and Publishing Inc.

Communication

- Egyptian language was written in three scripts: hieroglyphics, hieratic, and demotic.

- Hieroglyphics—form of picture writing with about 700 signs—was used for texts about history or religious beliefs.

- Hieroglyphics have provided scientists with information about ancient Egypt.

- Hieratic and demotic were used for business and everyday matters because they were easier to write.

- Hieratic was a simpler cursive script and was used regularly until about 800 B.C.

- Demotic was used in documents from the end of the 7th century B.C. It became the general form of writing for business, legal, and literary documents for nearly a thousand years, while hieroglyphics were used on stone inscriptions and hieratic for religious literature. Although developed from business hieratic, demotic had its own grammar and a new vocabulary.

- A Frenchman, Jean Francois Champollion, worked out how to read these languages using the Rosetta Stone, which is now in the British Museum in London. This stone had an inscription honoring King Ptolemy V written in Greek, hieroglyphic, and demotic.

- Papyrus paper, reed pens, and a palette were used for writing. A pen was dipped in a pot of gum and wriggled across a dry slab of red ink, then the gum and ink were mixed together on the palette.

Countryside

- Devised a system of irrigation.

- *Shaduf* was a lever and bucket that took the water from one level to another.

- Grew cereals, vegetables, and fruit.

- Kept animals (cows, sheep, goats, pigs, and poultry) for food and leather.

- Flax was grown to make linen for clothes.

- Papyrus plant provided writing paper, ropes, boats, sandals, and baskets.

- Most people worked on the land—they grew enough to feed themselves and others who did not work on the land.

Economics

- Taxes were paid in food and goods. Money was not used until 525 B.C.
- There was a market—exchanged goods, fruit, vegetables, animals, clothing, pottery, vases, and dishes.
- Scribes were important civil servants. They were in charge of building supplies, keeping lists of the work that had been done, and paying the workmen.

Education

- Usually, one son of a noble was taught to read and write and do mathematics.
- Between ages 4–14, boys and girls attended school together.
- They learned to read, write, and do mathematics.
- Those who were going to become doctors, lawyers, or scribes studied the sacred writing called hieroglyphics.
- Students had to copy out stories and religious writings.
- Children wrestled, played games, and learned to swim.
- When boys were 14, they followed their father's profession.
- Children learned to read by chanting and practiced writing model letters and exercises—some of these writings have survived.
- Exercises were intended not only to train the students to write but also were often copies of wise sayings to teach character.
- Also, there was instruction in mathematics, astronomy, astrology, and practical arts, sports, and games to train the character.
- Egyptians wanted to produce students who fit well into society—"Wisdom Literature," which survives, gives advice in the form of wise sayings from an older man to his pupil on how to behave and live correctly in society.

Food

- Teeth from mummies showed attrition (wearing away of outer surface of teeth).
- Cereals, barley, wheat, lentils, cucumbers, beans, leeks, onions, dates, figs, and grapes are among the foods eaten.
- Beef was a favorite meat but Egyptians also ate lamb, pork, goat, fish, duck, and goose.

- Basic foods for poorer people included bread, onions, other vegetables, and fruit.
- Rich people had more variety, including cakes sweetened with honey.

Geography

- In North Africa
- Northern shore of Mediterranean Sea
- Nile River
- Floods around river brought mud
- Ancient Egypt called "Kemet"—black land, color of the rich soil
- Land beyond ancient Egypt called "deshret" or "red land"
- Pyramids were built between the red and black lands
- Natural barriers: Mediterranean—north, Red Sea—east; tropical Africa—south. Natural barriers protected Egypt from foreign invasion and other cultural influences, which meant that a unique and distinctive civilization developed.
- Dryness and warmth of climate preserve monuments and artifacts.

Gods

- Prayed at home to gods.
- Adoration of animals and nature is found over and over again in the spiritual views of societies in which humans have felt themselves dominated by the forces in their environment.
- In the religion of the ancient Egyptians, the gods were at first represented in animal form; then, divinities began to take on human form with only the head preserving animal characteristics or, sometimes, merely one single animal attribute (horns) remained.
- Bes, a jolly dwarf-god, god of music and dancing.
- His wife, Tauert, the hippopotamus goddess.
- The Egyptians kept statues in their homes.
- Cat goddess, Bast, protected the home.
- Anubis, god of the dead, had the characteristics of a jackal and was god of embalming.
- Khnum, the prolific creator, was a ram.

- Thoth, the god of wisdom, was sometimes symbolized by an ibis and sometimes a baboon.
- Hathor, goddess of love and birth, had the appearance of the cow.
- The Egyptians did not worship just one single bull but rather three bulls chosen because of the particular coloration of their hides:

  a. Buchis, entirely white with a black head;

  b. Mnevis, a black coat sprinkled with spots shaped like ears of corn;

  c. Apis, black but distinctive because of two white spots of a special and definite shape—one a triangle on the forehead; the other, on the back, a crescent or a shape resembling a bird of prey with outstretched wings. Apis was a god of fruitfulness.

  When the bull died, it was placed in a sarcophagus replaced after 70 days.
- Sekhmet resembles a lioness.
- Thueris ensured fertility and birth and had the body of a hippopotamus.
- Horus, the god of sky, with falcon head, as the protector of the pharaoh
- Amon was the king of the gods.
- Ra, or Re, was the sun god (form of man with a falcon's head).
- Sobek was the crocodile god.
- Amon-Ra was a combined form of two gods.
- Temple gods were more important and received daily food from the priests.

History of Kingdoms
- Most knowledge about Egypt comes from the tombs, but the discovery of a town that was created to house those who built a Pharaoh's pyramid has revealed much.
- It is believed that many of the workers who built the pyramids were foreign. A technique called Neutron Activation of Analysis irradiated their remains in a reactor and obtained a breakdown of their various elements. The elements can then be compared with the composition of natural materials from Egypt and elsewhere.
- 6,000 years ago people in the Nile Valley began to develop the way of life we call ancient Egyptian.

SkyLight Training and Publishing Inc.

- Two kingdoms developed—one in the north called the "red land" and another in the south known as the "white land." Each had its own king.

- 5,000 years ago (3100 B.C.) the king of the south (Menes) conquered the north and Egypt was united.

- The north was called Lower Egypt.

- The south was called Upper Egypt.

- The whole country was called Kemet.

- Menes founded Egypt's first capital at Memphis. This is when Egypt became a kingdom.

- From 2800 B.C. to 2300 B.C., the pharaohs of the Old Kingdom reigned over prosperous land. Pepi I is believed to have reigned peacefully for 94 years. After Pepi's death, there was a period of unrest, which destroyed the peaceful unity of Egypt.

- Two cities—Heracleopolis and Thebes—maintained order in their areas. Thebes, a city in Upper Egypt, was victor and reunited the country. The Middle Kingdom lasted from 2050 B.C. to 1650 B.C. The new pharaohs of Thebes imposed on the country the worship of the god Amon, whom they associated with the ancient sun god of the first Egyptians.

- During this time, they dried out the swamps of the Fayum, southwest of Memphis, and acquired more than 10,000 acres for cultivation. Then, the Hyksos attacked and conquered Egypt. The Asian Hyksos introduced the Egyptians to war chariots harnessed to horses; they spread terror. However, the Hyksos were driven out by the pharaoh Kamose and, in 1590 B.C., the New Kingdom began.

- The third period of unity, from 1550 to 1100 B.C., was a time when pharaohs engaged in a policy of conquest.

- This is when the Egyptians became the masters of Palestine, Syria, and Nubia.

- But they were constantly in battle to defend conquests.

- From 1050 B.C. to 525 B.C., Egypt was unable to regain its former power and was divided politically. Egyptians became the prey of Assyrians, who seized Memphis and Thebes; Persians, who conquered the entire country; and then Greeks. The Romans, under Caesar, established themselves in Egypt during the time it was governed by Cleopatra.

- The ancient Egyptians were descended from hunters who lived in North Africa.

Houses

- Houses were built of mud brick and wood—ideal in a hot country with little rainfall.
- In well-established villages, houses were built close together and had two or more stories.
- In newer ones—sprawling villas were built.
- Even smaller houses often had four rooms with an outside courtyard—women cooked in courtyard in pottery ovens.

Kings

- Kings were called Pharaoh—comes from the words "per aa," which meant the great house or palace where he lived.
- Believed they were half god and half human and able to ask the gods for their blessing for themselves and all Egyptians.
- Believed the pharaoh was very important to Egypt's security and prosperity.
- Tutankhamun is the most famous. His is the only royal tomb in the Valley of the Kings that has been discovered almost untouched. (Found by archaeologist Howard Barter in 1922 after many years of digging.)
- Priest called Manetho—written piece of evidence of Egyptian history. He divided a list of kings into "dynasties."
- A dynasty usually includes rulers of one family—one is connected to his successor through family links, or a new dynasty is introduced when a king seizes the throne.
- Headings of dynasties:
  - Predynastic Period (c. 5000–c. 3100 B.C.)
  - Archaic Period (Dynasties 1 & 2, 3100–2686 B.C.)
  - Old Kingdom (Dynasties 3–6, 2686–2181 B.C.)
  - First Intermediate Period (Dynasties 7–11, 2181–1991 B.C.)
  - Middle Kingdom (Dynasty 12, 1991–1786 B.C.)
  - Second Intermediate Period (Dynasties 13–17, 1786–1552 B.C.)
  - New Kingdom (Dynasties 18–20, 1552–1069 B.C.)
  - Third Intermediate Period (Dynasties 21–26, 1069–525 B.C.)
  - Late Period (Dynasties 27–31, 525–332 B.C.)
  - Graeco–Roman Period (332 B.C.–A.D. 641)

- The great eras of Egyptian history were the Old, Middle, and New Kingdoms.
- Society of ancient Egypt was like a pyramid—top was king (head of army, navy, law courts, and state religion), then nobles (sometimes, members of a king's family; they owned land and property, were subject to king's favor, and held top posts in the government—sometimes, king limited their power), minor state officials (daily business of government—Treasury, the Civil Services, the Records Office), craftsmen (stonemasons; carpenters; jewelers; smiths employed on building, decorating, and equipping king's tomb), ordinary workers.
- Pharoah often married to own sibling—sister or brother.
- Audience with king held in reception hall of the palace.

Leisure

- Board game (like Parcheesi), called mehen or "serpent game." Players had 3 lions and 3 lionesses and little white and red balls, often made of ivory, which were kept in a little ebony box. Not known exactly how it was played.
- Some games had a social role to help players forget their quarrels.
- Music and dancing were popular.
- Nobles held banquets where large quantities of food and drink were served to guests and entertainment was provided by dancers.
- Some entertainers or dancers could also do acrobatics.
- Hunting was a popular pastime among the rich.

Marriage

- Married young—boys, 15, girls, 12.
- Young people chose their own partner.
- Marriages not arranged.
- Earliest love songs from Egypt.
- Some men married more than one wife—although the rich usually did not.

Medicine

- Most died in their 40s.
- Became ill from diseases caused by sand and water.

- Sand in air caused lung disease.

- Sand in bread wore down people's teeth.

- Worms in river water carried diseases.

- Had world's earliest medical profession.

- Doctors, nurses, and medical students were trained at the temples.

- Doctors performed operations and created medicines.

- Medicines were unpleasant to frighten away the evil spirit that was thought to cause illnesses.

- Treatments were recorded in ancient medical documents.

- Even attempted a cure for the common cold.

- Today scientists x-ray mummies, study blood groups, and examine their body tissue under a microscope.

Mummification

- The Egyptians believed that everyone had a soul and a body, and the body was needed after death because it fed the soul on the offerings of food left at the tomb. Therefore, tried to preserve the bodies (mummification).

- Craftsmen created jars (Canopic jars) that held the internal organs removed during the mummification.

- Used coffins before mummification, some basket and some pottery. Poor still used coffins after mummification. Later, tombs became more elaborate.

- Priests dressed in jackal mask of Anubis, god of cemeteries and mummification.

- Mummification developed around 2700 B.C.

- In early years, bodies were just buried in sand, where they dried out before decaying. Egyptians noticed this. When bodies were buried in tombs, they decayed before they dried out. Soon after first pyramid was built, Egyptians developed a chemical method called mummification to dry and preserve the body.

- The word comes from the Arabic word *mummia*, which means bitumen. Some of the later mummies have a blackened appearance as if they were covered in bitumen, so this name was wrongly applied to them but has survived.

- The only written accounts of mummification are by Greek historians Herodotus and Diodorus Siculus.
- Mummification took 70 days (30 for religious rites). The most expensive process involved the removal of the internal organs (viscera) through a cut in the stomach. Body and organs were treated with dry natron (a salt compound) to remove the fluids from the tissues. Organs were put in jars with heads, representing the four demi-gods, to protect them. The body was wrapped in layers of bandages, between which were inserted jewelry and amulets to bring magical protection.

Pets

- Dogs were important—placed on sarcophagi—but did not receive affection.
- Perhaps god of dead (jackal) was actually a dog.
- Monkeys were more favored than dogs and were sacred animals represented by Thoth, the god of wisdom. They were never punished.
- Geese were considered pets and wandered through the house. They were not even sacrificed to the gods.
- Most families had pets. Cats were the favorite because they killed rats and mice; but Egyptians also kept monkeys or birds as pets.
- Lioness Sekhmet, goddess of war, was succeeded by Bastet, the cat-goddess.
- Many Egyptians believed the cat was their ancestor. The women used makeup to give themselves a catlike look, and children were consecrated to Bastet by making a cut in an arm into which a priest poured several drops of cat's blood. When a cat died, the sorrow of its masters was so great they shaved off their eyebrows.
- Egyptians attempted to domesticate all sorts of animals—some were successful. Tried but were unsuccessful with hyenas and a breed of wolf. However, they were successful with oxen, donkeys, pigs, goats, and lambs (donkeys and pigs were considered impure).

Politics and Law

- Had efficient system of government.
- Took census in fields every two years and a census of the cattle.
- Had universal tax system; many were employed by the government to administer and collect the taxes.

- In theory, every citizen was obliged to work for the king on irrigation, building, and other projects when required, but the wealthy would buy off this obligation.

- In theory, the king owned everything in Egypt; therefore, the king could take anything from you.

- Slavery in which an individual has no legal rights was unknown but some groups of people could be owned, bought, sold to others, and legally set free. Even these people could own possessions, land, bequeath to their children, marry, and keep servants.

- Taxation provided much of the wealth the king needed.

- Law gave rich and poor the right to be heard but punishments were severe.

- People found guilty of capital offenses would be thrown to the crocodiles, losing their life and the chance of a proper burial for their body.

- Punishment could also be beatings or cutting off an ear or a nose.

- Whole families could be punished for a crime committed by one of its members.

Pyramids

- Pyramids first appeared during the Old Kingdom when Egyptian civilization produced many major new ideas.

- Used to bury kings.

- Built at the edge of the desert.

- Joined to the Nile by a long causeway.

- Furnished with a series of chambers.

- Decorated inside with texts, magical spells. "A ramp to the sky is built for him, that he may go up to the sky on it. He flies as a bird and he settles as a beetle on an empty seat that is in the ship of Re" (Rosalie and Antony David, *History as Evidence: Ancient Egypt*, Warwick Press, 1984, 12) The "ramp" is probably the pyramid.

- Large stone coffin—sarcophagus.

- Many were robbed, probably soon after king's burial, which is probably the reason Egyptians stopped building them—too easily plundered.

- British Egyptologist, Sir W. Flinders Petrie, discovered jewelry belonging to real princesses in tombs near the pyramid of King Sesostris II at Lahun.

- Some queens seem to have separate tombs, but small pyramids at Giza also may have been for this purpose. However, no remains have been found.

- Development of pyramid: step, bent pyramid, and true pyramid.

- Egyptians left no account of how pyramids were built.

- When the Nile flooded the land, peasants would work on pyramids rather than farming the land.

- Some stone was quarried locally—other stone (granite) was brought by river from Aswan, which was more than 500 miles to the south, and then dragged on rollers from the river to the pyramid site.

- Ramps were built to allow the men to drag the stones up to the work level.

- First, the core was built; then, limestone facing was applied, working from the top down to the ground. The ramps were removed as they worked downward.

Religion

- Egyptians were very religious.

- Artifacts on walls and small statues tell of their religion.

- Most priests only spent three months a year in the temple—the rest of the time, they were doctors, lawyers, or scribes and lived at home with their families.

- Gods played many different parts. Some were gods of nature, of the sun, moon, sky, and earth; others were gods of arts and crafts and healing; many were members of family groups.

- The temple was seen as the god's house, and the priests were servants to look after the god's needs.

- Priests had daily rituals—remove statue from shrine, remove clothing and makeup, and redress.

- Women were not allowed to become priests but could be singers and dancers at the temples. They sang to wake up the god everyday; this was called the Daily Temple Ritual.

- Festivals were held several times a year to amuse and entertain the gods.

- After entering the Next World, it was thought the dead person was brought before a group of judges. He had to assure them that he had led a good life. Then the jackal god Anubis weighed the person's heart against the Feather of Truth while other important gods looked on. If the heart was heavier than the feather, it meant the person had led a wicked life and would be eaten by a monster. If the heart was lighter, the person would enter a happy land and be greeted by all dead relatives and friends.

Resources and Trade

- Had a lot of gold.

- Not much wood—imported from Syria.

- Imported wood from Lebanon, metals from Asia, and incense from the land of Punt (exact location unknown—but on Red Sea, probably near what is Somaliland).

- Obtained silver, ostrich feathers, ebony, and ivory from Asia Minor, the Aegean Islands, and Nubia, part of present-day Sudan.

Scientific Contributions

- Time counted in years of 365 days thanks to their astronomers; weeks were 10 days long; and there were three weeks in a month. Seasons were divided into four months.

War

- Natural barriers protected Egypt from invasion so the Egyptians did not have to fight wars continuously.

- Nubians, who lived to the south, were colonized by Egypt because of their gold supply. Egyptians built a string of fortresses with thick brick walls.

- In 1600 B.C., Egypt was invaded by the Hyksos (from Asia) and this changed the Egyptian attitude toward war.

- After driving out the Hyksos, the Egyptians of the New Kingdom were more aggressive, with a policy of conquest in Syria and Palestine, and they continued to dominate Nubia. This was when the professional standing army was established.

- Weapons of the Old and Middle Kingdoms were slings, bows, spears, daggers, maces, axes, and leather or wooden shields. These were supplemented by others introduced by Hyksos—the horse and chariot, the curved sword, and more armor.

- The king was commander-in-chief and led his troops into battle.

- There were infantry but no cavalry and the navy was an auxiliary branch of the army-carrying troops and supplies. The navy was not used as a fighting force until the late New Kingdom.

Important Dates in Ancient Egypt*

Note: Most of these dates are so old that historians argue over the exact years. All dates are B.C.

3100	Upper and Lower Egypt united into one kingdom
3100–2686	The Early Dynastic Period
2860	Papyrus is first used for writing
2600	The first step pyramid is built for Pharaoh Djoser at Saqqarah
2686	The Old Kingdom (Dynasties III–IV)
	The Great pyramid is built at Giza during Dynasty IV
2325–2150	Trading is at its height
1991–1786	The Middle Kingdom (Dynasties XI and XII)
	During Dynasty XI the Egyptian Empire grows, especially to the south
	During Dynasty XII the arts flourish in Egypt
1680–1568	Invasion of the Hyksos and their rule of Egypt
1567–1085	The New Kingdom: Egyptian Empire at its largest
1361–1352	Rule of Pharaoh Tutankhamun
950–730	Dynasty XXII, when Egypt is ruled by Libyan kings
664–332	The Late Period, when Egypt is ruled by Persian and Ethiopian kings as well as Egyptian pharaohs. Dynasties XXV–XXX
332	Alexander the Great claims Egypt for Greece. Egypt is ruled by Greece and Macedonia until it becomes part of the Roman Empire in 30 B.C.

* Excerpt from R. Coote, *Look into the Past: The Egyptians* (New York, Thomson Learning, 1993).

Reference List

Barell, J. 1995. *Teaching for thoughtfulness: Classroom strategies to enhance intellectual development.* 2d ed. New York: Longman.

Bennett, H. G. 1953. *Innovation: The basis of cultural change.* New York: McGraw-Hill.

Bellanca, J. 1990. *The cooperative think tank.* Arlington Heights, IL: IRI/SkyLight Training and Publishing.

Boyce, L. N., J. VanTassel-Baska, J. D. Burruss, B. T. Sher, and D. T. Johnson. 1997. Problem-based curriculum: Parallel learning opportunities for students and teachers. *Journal for the Education of the Gifted* 20(4): 363–379.

Burke, K. 1993. *How to access authentic learning training manual.* Arlington Heights, IL: IRI/SkyLight Training and Publishing.

Cawley, C., D. T. Johnson, J. VanTassell-Baska, L. N. Boyce, and K. H. Hall. 1995. *Journeys and destinations: The challenge of change.* Saratoga Springs, NY: Washington-Saratoga-Warren-Hamilton-Essex BOCES and the Center for Gifted Education at the College of William and Mary.

Center for Gifted Education. 1994. *Language arts training manual.* Williamsburg, VA: College of William and Mary.

Center for Gifted Education, College of William and Mary. 1998. *Language arts units for high ability learners, K–8.* Dubuque, IA: Kendall Hunt.

Center for Gifted Education, College of William and Mary. In press. *Autobiographies.* Dubuque, IA: Kendall Hunt.

Fogarty, R. 1997. *Problem-based learning and other curriculum models for the multiple intelligences classroom.* Arlington Heights, IL: IRI SkyLight Training and Publishing.

Goodenough, W. H. 1963. *Cooperation in change; Anthropological approach to community change.* New York: Russell Sage Foundation.

Hugill, P. J., and D. B. Dickson. 1988. Introduction to *The transfer and transformation of ideas and material culture*, xi–xxii. College Station: Texas A & M University Press.

Smith, A. 1976. *Social change.* New York: Longman.

Spindler, L. S. 1977. *Culture change and modernization.* San Francisco, CA: Holt, Rinehart, and Winston.

Spindler, L. S., and G. D. Spindler. 1959. Culture change. In *Biennial review of Anthropology*, edited by B. J. Siegel. Stanford, CA: Stanford University Press.

VanTassel-Baska, J. 1994. *Comprehensive curriculum for gifted learners.* Boston: Allyn and Bacon.

VanTassel-Baska, J., D. T. Johnson, C. E. Hughes, and L. N. Boyce. 1996. A study of language arts curriculum effectiveness with gifted learners. *Journal for the Education of the Gifted* 19(4): 461–480.

White, L. 1959. *The evolution of culture.* New York: McGraw-Hill.

Woods, C. M. 1975. *Cultural change.* Dubuque, IA: Wm. C. Brown.

Index

Training and Publishing Inc.

We Prepare Your Teachers Today
for the Classrooms of Tomorrow

Learn from Our Books and from Our Authors!

Ignite Learning in Your School or District.

SkyLight's team of classroom-experienced consultants can help you foster systemic change for increased student achievement.

Professional development is a process, not an event. SkyLight's seasoned practitioners drive the creation of our on-site professional development programs, graduate courses, research-based publications, interactive video courses, teacher-friendly training materials, and online resources—call SkyLight Training and Publishing Inc. today.

SkyLight specializes in three professional development areas.

Specialty #

Best Practices

We **model** the best practices that result in improved student performance and guided applications.

Specialty #

Making the Innovations Last

We help set up **support** systems that make innovations part of everyday practice in the long-term systemic improvement of your school or district.

Specialty #

How to Assess the Results

We prepare your school leaders to encourage and **assess** teacher growth, **measure** student achievement, and **evaluate** program success.

Contact the SkyLight team and begin a process toward long-term results.

2626 S. Clearbrook Dr., Arlington Heights, IL 60005
800-348-4474 • 847-290-6600 • FAX 847-290-660
http://www.iriskylight.com

There are
one-story intellects,
two-story intellects, and three-story
intellects with skylights. All fact collectors, who
have no aim beyond their facts, are one-story men. Two-story men
compare, reason, generalize, using the labors of the fact collectors as
well as their own. Three-story men idealize, imagine,
predict—their best illumination comes from
above, through the skylight.

—*Oliver Wendell*

Holmes

SkyLight
Training and Publishing Inc.